GU00792247

Penthouse Living

Published in Great Britain in 2005 by Wiley-Academy,
a division of John Wiley & Sons Ltd

Copyright © 2005

John Wiley & Sons Ltd, The Atrium, Southern Gate, Chichester,
West Sussex PO19 8SQ, England

Telephone (+44) 1243 779777

Email (for orders and customer service enquiries): cs-books@wiley.co.uk

Visit our Home Page on www.wileyeurope.com or www.wiley.com

All Rights Reserved. No part of this publication may be reproduced, stored
in a retrieval system or transmitted in any form or by any means, electronic,
mechanical, photocopying, recording, scanning or otherwise, except under
the terms of the Copyright, Designs and Patents Act 1988 or under the
terms of a licence issued by the Copyright Licensing Agency Ltd, 90
Tottenham Court Road, London W1T 4LP, UK, without the permission in
writing of the Publisher. Requests to the Publisher should be addressed to
the Permissions Department, John Wiley & Sons Ltd, The Atrium, Southern
Gate, Chichester, West Sussex PO19 8SQ, England, or emailed to
permreq@wiley.co.uk, or faxed to (+44) 1243 770571.

This publication is designed to provide accurate and authoritative
information in regard to the subject matter covered. It is sold on the
understanding that the Publisher is not engaged in rendering professional
services. If professional advice or other expert assistance is required, the
services of a competent professional should be sought.

Other Wiley Editorial Offices

John Wiley & Sons Inc., 111 River Street, Hoboken, NJ 07030, USA

Jossey-Bass, 989 Market Street, San Francisco, CA 94103-1741, USA

Wiley-VCH Verlag GmbH, Boschstr. 12, D-69469 Weinheim, Germany

John Wiley & Sons Australia Ltd, 33 Park Road, Milton, Queensland 4064,
  Australia

John Wiley & Sons (Asia) Pte Ltd, 2 Clementi Loop #02-01, Jin Xing
  Distripark, Singapore 129809

John Wiley & Sons Canada Ltd, 22 Worcester Road, Etobicoke, Ontario,
  Canada M9W 1L1

ISBN: 0470094494   UPC: 723812740741

Layout and Prepress: ARTMEDIA PRESS LTD, London

Printed and bound by Conti Tipocolor, Italy

Penthouse Living

Jonathan Bell

Series Designer **Liz Sephton**

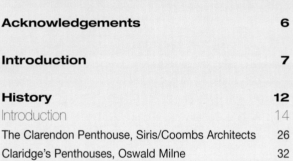

contents

I would like to thank Mr Carter B. Horsley, The City Review, www.thecityreview.com, Christopher Stocks, all the architects and photographers who provided the images, but especially Michael Frantzis and Andreas Gehrke, as well as Helen Castle and Famida Rasheed at John Wiley, and last, but not least, Alex Adie.

Acknowledgements

Photographic Credits
The author and publisher gratefully acknowledge the following for permission to reproduce material in the book. While every effort has been made to contact copyright holders for their permission to reprint material in this book the publishers would be grateful to hear from any copyright holder who is not acknowledged here and will undertake to rectify any errors or omissions in future editions.

Cover: © Chris Gascoigne/VIEW/ Simon Conder; pp 1 & 172–3 © Ora-Ito; pp 2–3 © Keith Parry; pp 4(l), 98–105 Paul Harmer; pp 4(r) & 120–3 © Monty Gershon, photos: Richard Leeney; pp 5(tr) & 90–5 © Leon Chew; pp 5(bl), 10, 186–7, 188(b) & 189(b) © Richard Hywel Evans Architecture and Design Ltd, photos: Guy Drayton; pp 8–9 & 63–5 'Playboy's Patio Terrace' (August 1963). Reproduced by Special Permission of Playboy Magazine. Copyright © 1963 by Playboy. All rights reserved; p 11 & 200–5 © Werner Aisslinger, photos: Steffen Jänicke; pp 12–3, 16 & 26–31 © Jane Siris, photos: Jennifer Krogh Photography; p 15, 48–9 & 210–11 © Michael Frantzis; p 19 © James Wagman Architect, LLC; p 21 © Helena Rubinstein Foundation; p 22 © The Dorchester Hotel; p 23 © Manhattan Loft Corporation; pp 24–5 © Kensington Roof Gardens; pp 33–7 & 50–3 © RIBA Library Photographs Collection; pp 38–9 & 70–5 © Harry Seidler, photos: Eric Sierens; p 41 © Guard Tillman Pollock, photo: Tony Chan; pp 42–3 © Norman McGrath Photographer, Inc.; pp 45 & 67–9 Richard Bryant/arcaid.co.uk; p 46 © Craig Kellogg; p 47 © TC Communications; pp 54–7 © Munkenbeck + Marshall Architects; pp 58–9 & 63 'Playboy Penthouse Apartment' (September 1956). Reproduced by Special Permission of Playboy Magazine. Copyright © 1956 by Playboy. All rights reserved; pp 60–2 'Playboy Town House' (May 1962). Reproduced by Special Permission of Playboy Magazine. Copyright © 1962 by Playboy. All rights reserved; pp 79–82 & 84–6 © Raimund Koch; p 83 © Jonathan Bell; pp 88–9 © Johannes Saurer, photos: Christine Blaser; pp 76–7, 107(t), 108–9 & 112–3 Tadao Ando Architect & Associates; pp 107(b), 110 & 115 © Tomio Ohashi; pp 117–9 © Chris Gascoigne/VIEW/ Simon Conder; p 125 © 1999 Eric Staudenmaier; pp 126–9 © Loh architects; pp 131–3 © Dennis Gilbert/VIEW/Blauel Architects; pp 134–9 © Winka Dubbeldam. Inc.; pp 140–1 © Open Building Research; pp 142–5 © Paul Cha + Margaret Innerhofer; pp 146–9 © Martin Finio; pp 150 & 152(b) © Pierre d'Avoine Architects; pp 151(t), 153(b), 154 & 155 © Gregory Ross; pp 151(b), 152(t) & 153(t) © David Grandorge; pp 156–7 © Alan Williams; pp 158 & 160–3 © First Penthouse Limited, photos: Eva Edsjö; pp 159 & 161 © Ian Macaulay; p 167 (t) © Tangram Architekten BV; p 167 (b), © MVRDV; p 168 © Marks Barfield Architects; p 169 © FAT; p 171(t+r) © LOT-EK; p 171(l+b) © Zedfactory Limited; p 174 © Stefan Horitsch/Klement Wassner; pp 176–7 courtesy Skidmore, Owings & Merrill, photos © Miller Hare; pp 178 –81 © SITE Environmental Design; pp 182–5 © dECOi; p 189 (t) © Richard Hywel Evans Architecture + Design Ltd, photo: Tom Foster; pp 164–5 & 190–5 © Rupert Steiner; pp 197–9 © Hertha Hurnaus; pp 209–6 © m-house; pp 212–3 © m3 architects.

The word 'penthouse' traditionally evokes the high life, an apartment with an undeniable aura of domestic exclusivity. To live in a penthouse is to be at the apex of domestic aspiration, to enjoy the most dramatic form of architecture yet devised. The penthouse is perceived as an elitist, elevated world whose owners can see everything from their lofty vantage point yet are themselves barely visible from the less privileged position of the street. Yet for exactly these reasons, 'penthouse' is also one of the most debased and misused words in architecture and urban design. This most saleable of words has become common currency in descriptions of contemporary apartment buildings the world over, the focus for an architecture of envy.

For nearly a century, penthouse living has remained inspirational and largely unattainable, thanks to the relative scarcity of space in the sky coupled with a high media profile that inflates prices still further. A penthouse is the ultimate urban location, perceived as the home of film stars, media moguls and captains of industry, or the setting for countless films and novels and the location of glittering A-list parties and elite social gatherings. The word penthouse conjures up an image of New York's so-called 'white-glove buildings', presided over by uniformed

Introduction

doormen and maintained by armies of invisible staff. In certain sections of New York society, the word still has enormous cachet – this is a city where a penthouse can span three or more floors, such as the $40 million triplex overlooking Central Park atop the Ritz Carlton Hotel that went on the market in early 2004.

Penthouses have been suffused with glamour since the first ones were built in the late 19th century. And the word itself soon became shorthand for a certain type of lifestyle, one with an undeniably sexual edge. In the 1950s and 1960s, *Playboy* magazine published a series of designs for its very own penthouse, roof terrace and town house, all of which featured expansive city views, presenting themselves as the epicentre of the urban bachelor experience. More famously, the word was appropriated wholesale by publisher Bob Guccione for his own top-shelf publication. Launched in 1965, *Penthouse* was differentiated from *Playboy* by the desire to push the boundaries of taste and decency still further. *Penthouse*'s notoriety ensured the word became associated with a whiff of perversion and the lure of the illicit (although Guccione himself favoured a town house, one of Manhattan's largest private houses, rather than a penthouse of his own).

Illicit thrills aside, the penthouse also has connotations of mystery and power; it is an urban stronghold, an unassailable fortress. Towards the end of his life, the billionaire Howard Hughes moved from penthouse suite to penthouse suite, surrounding himself only with acolytes and simply buying up the whole hotel if the management disapproved of his presence. Most famously, in 1966 Hughes owned the Las Vegas Desert Inn Hotel, where he reputedly remained for four years, the windows of the penthouse suite blacked out against the harsh desert sun.

No doubt the spires of contemporary Manhattan continue to harbour eccentric recluses, but in a media-saturated world, playing up your penthouse is more important than privacy. The latter-day mogul needs the penthouse as a psychological prop, one more weapon in the arsenal of big business, whether it's Donald Trump's elaborately overfurnished home on Fifth Avenue, the jewel of his property empire, or Rupert Murdoch's triplex on the city's Prince Street. Trump's penthouse took a small but highly visible role in the NBC reality television show *The Apprentice* (2004), on display as a gilded carrot to tempt a group of aspiring tycoons to great achievement. The same apartment had a small cameo in *The Devil's Advocate* (1997), treading a fine line between high camp and kitsch, yet clearly the epitome of the populist view of what a penthouse should be.

In books, films and television shows, the use of a vast apartment with extensive views has almost become a cliché, a convenient shorthand for vast power and wealth, and a useful source of photogenic vistas. Thrillers such as *Ransom* (1996), with its Central Park location (although the actual penthouse was a studio-based set, as was Anthony Hopkins's character's vast Manhattan triplex in *Meet Joe Black* (1998), complete with pool), use the elevated vantage point of the penthouse to highlight the character's importance, raising him or her above the prosaic. The imminent future world of *Minority Report* (2002) gave the protagonist an apartment that afforded him dramatic views over a futuristic cityscape, as well as being integrated into the city's transport system. In Ayn Rand's novel *The Fountainhead*, first published in 1936, the position of the penthouse, elevated far above the everyday and mundane, is a suitable metaphoric fit with the author's personal credo of self-determination and individualism.

Discussion of penthouse style could revolve forever around the facts, figures, prices and square footages that circulate in the upper echelons of the international property market. Yet, as current trends show, a precise definition of the term is elusive. Arguably, and for the purposes of *Penthouse Living*, a penthouse is a high-rise apartment – preferably at the very top of its building – with the benefit of extensive terraces or other outdoor space. A view is essential for the penthouse truly to live up to its name, and this view should have some impact upon the arrangement of the internal spaces.

It is tempting to describe a penthouse as a Modernist villa transported to a rooftop, but the very first penthouses were integrated architectural statements rather than stylistically different additions to a structure. Penthouses weren't villas, they were mansions, lording it over their surroundings. The word is now far more fluidly interpreted. Penthouse is all too often coupled with style, implying a space that takes elements of top floor living and applies them instead to a relatively standard apartment. These elements might be as simple as the copious use of glass or the provision of an outside terrace, however meagre. The requirement that a penthouse be on the upper floors of a building has long gone. In the 1990s

'PLAYBOY'S PATIO TERRACE' PLAYBOY MAGAZINE (AUGUST 1963, PP 98–9). ARTIST: HUMEN TAN

the purchaser of what had been advertised as a penthouse apartment, at the White House in London's Waterloo, developed from the former Shell Downstream office building, instigated a lawsuit when he discovered that the developers were constructing an additional two floors on the roof above his flat.

Like the loft, the penthouse has become ubiquitous, as the term is applied to ever more apartments. It no longer need mean the apex of a tower – penthouses can exist on all the upper floors, should the realtor or developer so decide. The term penthouse also acts as a class signifier; many of the pioneering New York lofts had huge terraces, commanding urban views and ample interior space, yet their industrial heritage precluded the use of the term penthouse, with its connotations of wealth, privilege, central location and physical aloofness from the world. The creative types who thrived in the spatially unfettered, highly flexible – and often illegally occupied – spaces of early loft culture simply chose not to make the association. Lofts were for artists; penthouses were for their patrons. Likewise, there was little room for edgy industrial glamour and materials in the traditional penthouse. Instead, the true penthouse frequently demonstrates extreme purity of vision and engineering in order to sustain its lofty perch.

Above: **Studio Aisslinger, LoftCube, Berlin, 2004.**

But, as we shall see, there is a difference between the penthouse as upper storey apartment and the architecturally distinct construction that sits on top of a building – perhaps even as a later addition to the structure. The emphasis on the penthouse as stand-alone object, an after-market item that can be retrospectively added, utilising architectural know-how and prefabricated components, is one of the main thrusts of the book – which shows examples of this approach and explains situations where a similar approach might be taken. This add-on architecture has also had implications for commercial buildings and property development, opening up new vistas and opportunities. There has subsequently arisen the almost oxymoronic term 'penthouse loft', the marrying of these two iconic urban architectural forms. Many architects confuse matters by blurring the terms still further, opening up the traditionally introverted world of the loft into the city at large.

The penthouse is a classification neglected in most orthodox architectural histories, perhaps on account of its perceived elitism or frivolity, neither of which is a trait that especially endears itself to the strictly Modernist approach taken to the history of architecture throughout the 20th century. The traditional architectural approach taken by the great apartment – and hotel – builders of late 19th- and early 20th-century New York is dismissed as mere styling, not innovation. These buildings achieved a sense of awe only through scale, and their applied decoration and shameless aping of French chateaux or medieval halls were sneered at by the dogmatic Modernists. Yet the lives lived in these hidden structures were hugely influential, filtering down through popular culture to stoke mass desire. As a result, the penthouse remains at the forefront of the popular imagination, one more magical ingredient in the appeal of the urban roofscape.

Opposite: **Richard Hywel Evans Architecture and Design Docklands Penthouse, London, 2003.**
View of the main living space

History

The penthouse has evolved into a living space for the urban elite. Yet this designation is paradoxical – how could the skyscraper, that most visible symbol of a supposedly democratic movement, International Modernism, culminate in such an elitist space? Modern architecture was about space, light and views for all, not just the privileged few.

Perhaps it's because the traditional penthouse actually predates 20th-century architecture's first attack of conscience. Originally, long before the elevator ushered in the vertical city, higher rooms meant a higher climb and rooftops, lofts and attics were the leftovers of real estate, thought suitable only for the serving classes (the arrangement of, for instance, the traditional English country house bears this out, with servants' quarters confined to cramped roof spaces). In this inverted past, the roofs of the city thrived as open spaces for the serving classes, providing sun and air in stark contrast to cramped and airless working-class streets. Laundry houses, maids' rooms and washing lines jostled with water towers, chimneypots and advertising hoardings. Penthouse comes from the Middle English *pentis* (with roots in the Latin *appendre*, which means 'to cause to be suspended') and initially applied

History

to the shed-like structures appended to existing buildings, little more than lean-tos. Gradually, *penthouse* evolved into the description of the rooftop housing for a stair or lift shaft, before its present meaning, that of the very top floor of an apartment building, entered popular usage.

The elevator brought symbolism and prestige to height: tall buildings afforded their architect, owner and occupier a certain status. In Chicago, which had suffered a devastating fire in 1871, the work of William Le Baron and Louis Sullivan and firms like Burnham & Root and Holabird & Roche rapidly convinced the burgeoning industrial elite that commercial operations belonged at the top of the world, looking down on all that they owned, operated, directed and created. The modern safety elevator – complete with the failsafe mechanism that supported the car should the cable snap – had been introduced by Elisha Otis in 1853. The German Werner von Siemens introduced an electrically operated elevator in 1880, and the industry is still dominated by companies bearing the names of these two innovators. The new Chicago was rebuilt as a vertical city, its clusters of warehouses and offices incorporating pioneering iron, steel and concrete construction to capitalise on the limited availability of real estate.

The overriding emphasis in the early years of building tall was on the facade and the massing; buildings of the era were chunky, tough statements, all rough-cut stone facades and brutally abrupt top-floor treatments derived from the classical pediment. The elements of the Beaux Arts style adopted by most of post-fire Chicago were continually adapted and teased into vertical form. Sullivan in particular was concerned with how the new breed of skyscrapers would meet the sky, proposing double-height upper storeys, ornamental friezes and pediments. Adler & Sullivan's 1891 proposal for the Mercantile Club of St Louis is a precursor of the New York apartment buildings of the 20th century; a plain office is topped by a vast mansarded and colonnaded mansion in the sky. The master of building tall clearly knew which part of the building was the most prestigious. Louis Sullivan and Dankmar Adler's masterpiece, the Chicago Auditorium of 1887–9, was a virtuoso multifunctional space, containing the auditorium theatre, an office complex and a large hotel, one of the earliest high-rise examples. It was followed by other hotels, including Starrett and Fuller's Hyde Park Hotel, a modest eight storeys but with luxurious five-roomed suites, complete with private baths, steam heating and incandescent lighting. Partitions enabled the sizeable rooms to be subdivided as necessary, an early venture into transformable space.

Although the Chicago School architects were primarily concerned with commercial buildings, the apartment also rose in popularity in the city, as similar technologies were applied and the way of life afforded by a central location was seen to be preferable to house ownership ('the modern flat is the palace of those who wish to be relieved of house owning and its cares', noted the author of *Industrial Chicago* in 1884;[1] strong parallels can be drawn with exhortations from today's volume apartment builders anxious to sell the maximum number of units possible on the premise of improved lifestyle). As the reliance on a structural external frame increased, so did window sizes, enabling tall structures to have unprecedented floor to ceiling windows.

To an even greater extent than Chicago, New York symbolised the modern American cityscape, an architectural vision unlike anything Europe had ever seen. From the late 19th century onwards, the city's financial district, focusing on Wall Street and Broad Street, home to insurance companies and financial institutions for a hundred years, gradually extended upwards. By the 1920s,

Right: New York roofscape, 2003. The space above the city offers almost unlimited architectural uses

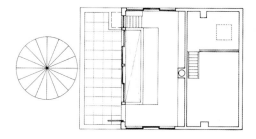

Architect's Penthouse   Siris/Coombs Architects   Manhattan, 1983

If Siris/Coombs's conversion of the 1908 Clarendon Penthouse (see page 26) epitomises the contemporary approach to New York's classic structures, the penthouse Jane Siris and Peter Coombs constructed, over a long period and on a considerably smaller budget, illustrates the other side of rooftop living.

The Architect's Penthouse exploits the last scraps of urban real estate in the heart of the city, the air rights that dance above the flat-roofed commercial structures and lesser apartments, buildings not deemed important enough to be crowned with terraces and spires. The original site consisted of three small rooms for maids and a laundry room, the typical rooftop contents of a turn of the century apartment. 'It was an opportunity to build three-dimensionally in New York,' says Siris, recalling the absence of vacant lots upon which a young firm could build and describing the rooftops of Manhattan as 'land in the air'. In the city, rooftop architecture was the last bastion of external expression, as the craze for loft living and the absence of plots meant that a whole generation of architects internalised their output.

Yet the Architect's Penthouse is anything but inward-looking. A modestly sized, three-storey monopitched structure, Siris/Coombs's own penthouse perches on the edge of the rooftop, allowing for a slender sliver of terrace at the front. 'Living on the 12th floor was like having a private house,' says Siris, commenting that the terrace contained such suburban accoutrements as a swing, sandbox and barbecue. The multilayered internal spaces are equally modest in size, a world away from the rooftop McMansions that crowd nearby air space. The built-in furniture and open-plan arrangement serve to create more visual space in what is otherwise a relatively cramped floor plan.

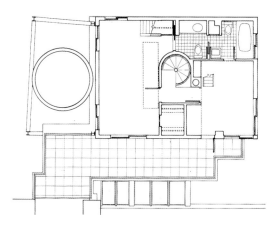

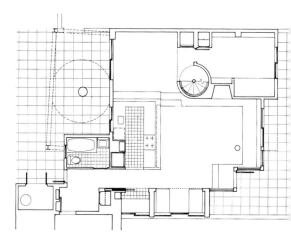

company headquarters were regularly exceeding 20 storeys in height, spurred on by Mr Otis's invention, the structural excellence of the steel frame, the economic need for more space and the romance of height. Towers began to terminate with peaks and towers, new spires for the religion of finance. New spaces with new, hitherto unseen views were created, architecturally distinct from the slender, stone-clad columns they topped. To inhabit one of these spaces was, architects realised, to be at the very summit of the city.

The emphasis on height in the commercial property market (epitomised by the well-publicised battle between the developers of the Chrysler Building and the Empire State Building in the late 1920s, and the earlier quest of Henry L Doherty, president of the Cities Service Company, to crown Wall Street with the nation's most dramatic building) slowly filtered down to the residential market, and the roofscape was swiftly transformed. New York, naturally, was at the forefront of this movement, the birthplace of the modern penthouse, the vertical city that realised the expressive potential of height and the sheer delights of living in the clouds.

At first came the industrial barons, men (and they were all men) who spent their working lives in these peaks of commerce. It was appropriate, too, that they should live on high. Doherty, whose State Street penthouse (atop one of his commercial buildings) contains offices, gym, squash courts and laboratories, planned an even grander, higher space atop the new Cities Services Building (now AIG), completed in 1932. Although the ailing businessman never inhabited it, the 66th floor contained an observation gallery which eventually became a public gallery. Nonetheless, his architects, Clinton & Russell and Holton & George, did him proud, creating a striking pencil-thin tower atop a stepped ziggurat base. There was no room here for rooftop service areas or lines of drying washing. The fluted elevations terminated in a series of aluminium-balconied terraces, breezy eyries for the elite.

Captains of industry demanded a place in the sky, symbolically rising above the empires they commanded. Boardrooms and offices were elaborate fantasies, imitating baronial castles, colonial architecture or showcasing the latest sleek modern furniture. Work spaces aside, exclusive social spaces such as the Cloud Club, a members-only club located on the 66th to 68th floors of the Chrysler Building, an Art Deco masterpiece buried inside the gleaming spire, only served to add to the penthouse myth (the club was even rumoured to function as a high-class speakeasy during Prohibition), as did the elaborate sets and backdrops created by the Californian film studios. These presented a cinematic perfection unattainable in real life, but swiftly imitated by New York's developers and hoteliers who continued to shape this most cinematic of cities in the manner to which it had become accustomed.

Corporate one-upmanship aside, the residential penthouse was born from a combination of legislation and media popularisation. In 1916, new building codes for New York's escalating skyline stipulated the introduction of the setback facade, an attempt to avoid dark, lightless streets. Typically, a commercial building could rise vertically for a distance equivalent to two and a half times the width of the street it stood on. Above this it could rise much further, if the facade was set back 'one foot for each vertical rise equal to its height district factor multiplied by two'.[2] This system spurred architectural creativity and numerous ziggurat-like structures, festooned with terraces, erupted from the sidewalks.

Apartment buildings were designed in a similar idiom, replacing the earlier classically proportioned apartments, elaborate palaces which were little more than grossly overscaled versions of the Fifth Avenue mansions which they in turn had replaced. The new structures offered unprecedented possibilities. Roofs became increasingly elaborate, miniature cities with towers, minarets, terraces, pavilions and elaborate ornamentation. It was a different world, high above the streets, where anything seemed possible. The 1930s apartments at 1040 Fifth Avenue, designed by Rosario Candela, were topped with a yellow brick penthouse, with arched windows, a loggia and towering buttresses. Elsewhere, miniature temples, Gothic spires, stepped terraces and elaborate mansards were created.

The race was on to create bigger and better penthouse spectaculars, as the super-rich did deals with developers, tearing down their mansions and erecting vast apartment buildings in their place. In 1925, the fabulously named Marjorie Merriweather Post Hutton created one of the city's most remarkable residences, a 54-room triplex apartment atop the building at 1107 Fifth Avenue. Hutton, the General Foods 'cereal heiress', had previously lived in a town house on the site (as well as owning the site next door), and agreed to sell on the condition that the developer effectively recreate her extensive house on the summit of the new 14-storey structure. According to Andrew Alpern,[3] it was served by a private carriage driveway on 92nd Street and a private elevator as well as a separate ground-floor suite for a concierge. The apartment included a silver room, a wine room and cold storage rooms for flowers and furs along with a self-contained suite of rooms for Mrs Hutton's parents, Mr and Mrs Post. The penthouse was subsequently subdivided into six apartments and with time the grandeur has faded, if only slightly.

By 1925, when Emery Roth and Carrère & Hastings completed New York's Ritz Tower, then the tallest residential building in the world, the stepped ziggurat profile of New York's skyline was an internationally recognisable landscape of plateaus, peaks and terraces, celebrated in cinema and popular culture. 'For what is a penthouse terrace, ultimately,' wrote James Sanders in *Celluloid Skyline*, his compelling history of New York in the films, 'if not a platform from which to be launched on a magical journey above the city?'[4] Sanders noted the cinematic predilection for setting dramatic and romantic scenes in this most picturesque of locations. The glamour and scale of New York on the silver screen were almost entirely reconstructed, he noted; a parade of sets, back lots, studios and matte paints that fixed an unshakeable image of the penthouse in the public's consciousness. Hollywood's rooms

Opposite: **Lower East Side Penthouse.** Designed by James Wagman Architects. These images, which pre-date the destruction of the World Trade Center, illustrate a New York roofscape free from any anxiety, a garden in the sky that, for just a short while longer, would be a retreat from the pressures of city life

with a view are, inevitably, a phantom. From the sweeping city backdrop of Hitchcock's *Rope* to the more intimate cityscape that played such an integral role in the director's *Rear Window*, through to the grand rooftop mansions created for films like *Ransom* and *Meet Joe Black*, or the terraces of *Green Card*, these are penthouses and rooftops that exaggerate an already improbable reality. Sanders commented on how:

> the filmic city abounded in penthouses, to the point where it might seem as though anyone who didn't live in a tenement lived in a glamorous rooftop apartment … At the expressive level (which so often governed the shape of the film city) there was some kind of sense to this: Why have these tall buildings in the first place if some great reward could not be achieved at their tops?[5]

One of the earliest real penthouses to receive widespread media coverage belonged, appropriately enough, to a publisher. Condé Nast's penthouse at 1040 Park Avenue occupied the entire top floor of the building and was decorated by the flamboyant Elsie de Wolf, one of the very first celebrity interior designers. Nast was a legendary party-giver and threw a widely reported house-warming on 18 January 1925, his guests including the dancer Fred Astaire, composer George Gershwin and photographer Edward Steichen.[6] In the popular imagination, the line between Hollywood's patently false (though visually stunning) glamour and the real life of the stars was forever blurred.

The conflation of celebrity, fortune and the penthouse was good box office. Helena Rubinstein, the founder of the cosmetics company, owned a 26-room triplex penthouse at 625 Park Avenue for three decades. Almost completely enveloped by a series of terraces, the centrepiece of the six-bedroom apartment was a 20.75 metre (68 foot) long salon, a New World version of the salons created by European royalty in an earlier era. Another of Rubinstein's rooms was dedicated to Salvador Dalí's three *Fantastic Landscape* murals. Rubinstein died in 1965 and the apartment was bought by her competitor Charles Revson of Revlon, who lived there for a decade before his death in 1975.[7] In 1994, the apartment sold for $15 million, then a city record.

The lure of a so-called 'White Glove Building' (where the uniform code of the ubiquitous doorman or concierge stipulates immaculate white gloves) remains high. Today, there are still a few penthouse apartments of comparable grandeur and scale, but they are usually long hidden from public view, occasionally surfacing in the glossiest real estate publications, with price tags that are the talk of the gossip columns. These are tantalising glimpses of mysterious beasts, long thought extinct. The financier and art collector Saul Steinberg's penthouse at 740 Park Avenue was reported to have sold for $35 million in 2003. A triplex apartment on the 1930s building, designed in the classic stepped ziggurat style by one of the masters of New

Opposite: **Helena Rubinstein Penthouse.**
Decorated in the manner of a lofty country house or chateau, the penthouse offered a New World version of salon culture

Below: **Roof Garden Suites.** Champagne on the terrace of one of the Dorchester's four celebrated Roof Garden Suites. In London, the grand hotels of the Victorian and Edwardian era were among the few places to match the soaring glamour achieved across the Atlantic

Above: London's skyline. For centuries, London's residential culture was resolutely ground-based, leaving towers to the armies of office workers. In recent years, the idea of rooftop living has taken seed

York apartment building, Sicilian-born architect Rosario Candela, Steinberg's penthouse was around 1,858 square metres (20,000 square feet). Other comparable spaces include the Fairfax apartment in the Pierre Hotel, a 1,114 square metre (12,000 square foot) neo-French chateau with a 260 square metre (2,800 square foot) grand salon and several terraces overlooking Central Park. The fates of these structures rise and fall with the stock market or the notoriety of their occupants.

Where were the European equivalents? Centuries-old city fabric did not lend itself well to such reinvention. Indeed, in the first half of the 20th century, Europe appeared to hold upper storey living in distain. There was a dearth of such apartments in prominent developments in Europe's major cities as the older building stock, lack of physical stature and social structures were less receptive to the upturned world of penthouse living than their relatively young American counterparts. Consider an iconic building like Antonio Gaudí's celebrated Casa Milà in Barcelona, the upscale apartment building constructed from 1905 to 1907. Casa Milà's famously allegorical roofscape and huge, cave-like attics (now an exhibition space) brilliantly blend the city's skyline with that of the surrounding landscape, drawing on the tradition of the accessible, working rooftop in the tradition of the classic atrium-centric apartment building. Yet at the time of the Casa's construction, even the wealthiest patron would have considered it unthinkable to live in such a space.

In Paris, too, the attic was the domain of the artist, the romantic garret of legend, greatly removed from the opulent formal rooms on the lower storeys of the grander town houses. Certainly, London's high society had no chance of keeping up with the scale of these developments. The rash of interwar apartment building was modest in comparison with transatlantic developments, yet new ideas for living were spearheaded by development. In London, the architect Oswald Milne's penthouse suite at Claridge's hotel for

Above and opposite: Kensington Roof Gardens.
Laid out in 1936-8 by the landscape architect Ralph
Hancock on the roof of the Derry and Toms
department store, the gardens cover 0.6 hectares
(1.5 acres), 30 metres (100 feet) above the street,
incorporating rocks shipped in from Pennsylvania, 500
species of plants and shrubs and an eco-system that
has grown to include flamingos and ducks

the daughter of Richard D'Oyly Carte is a fine example of the more modest scale of construction in Britain. Stylish, yet also sober and unshowy.

Although the word penthouse has been debased by lesser imitators, cramped apartments that cannot hope to live up to their forebears, the penthouse apartment still represents the peak of aspiration. New-build apartments, whether they be retro-styled, like Michael Graves's 425 Fifth Avenue, which deliberately exploits the historical associations of the setback form to evoke a golden age of high-rise architecture, or sleekly modern, invariably promise a penthouse (or penthouses). But there is a distinct difference between the bespoke penthouse and the architectural experiment, between the space earmarked from the start of construction for a high-flyer and the hidden, unpromising rooftop site that was a struggle to discover, finance and construct. There was also the introduction of the loft and, for a time, both the classic penthouse and the rooftop experiment were out of favour as experimentation looked inwards, changing the internal landscapes of the apartment, rather than its relationship to the external world.

Notes
1   Siegfried Giedion, *Space, Time and Architecture*, Harvard University Press (Cambridge, Mass), third edition, 1956, p 375.
2   Daniel M Abramson, *Skyscraper Rivals: The AIG Building and the Architecture of Wall Street*, Princeton Architectural Press (New York), 2001, p 13.
3   Cited in *New York's Fabulous Luxury Apartments with Original Floor Plans from the Dakota, River House, Olympic Tower and other Great Buildings*, Dover Publications, 1987, quoted in *The City Review*, www.thecityreview.com
4   James Sanders, *Celluloid City*, Knopf (New York), 2001, p 103.
5   *Ibid*, p 245.
6   Christopher Gray, *The New York Times*, 7 November 1993, cited in *The City Review*.
7   James Trager, *Park Avenue, Street of Dreams*, Atheneum (New York), 1990.

Clarendon Penthouse

Siris/Coombs Architects

New York 1908, refurbished 1997

The Clarendon Penthouse is a remarkable survivor of New York's first era of grand penthouses and apartments, reconfigured and refurbished for a new century. The upper storeys of the 1908 Clarendon Apartments were originally the New York home of media tycoon William Randolph Hearst. It started with 30 rooms spread over a modest three floors, which expanded to five as Hearst wrested control of the entire 12-storey building away from a landlord unwilling – or too slow – to approve the tycoon's expansion plans.

Expansion took the form of a new copper-roofed mansard, a striking structure visible from across the broad Hudson River. Inside, 9 metre (30 foot) ceiling heights earned the 232 square metre (2,500 square foot) space the nickname 'tapestry gallery', a place for the famously avid collector's assorted tapestries, suits of armour, paintings, carpets and more. Following Hearst's eventual retreat with his mistress Marion Davies to the ersatz castle designed for him by Julia Morgan at San Simeon, the Clarendon Apartments were chopped up into more manageable sizes. The elaborate interiors were ripped out, the mansard lost its high ceiling and the upper section of the structure was effectively sealed off from the apartment building below.

In later years, this copper-clad island, adrift on a sea of empty rooftops, became an artist's studio, accessible only via a lonely (if spectacular) rooftop walk. The current owner acquired an empty shell and set about transforming it into an apartment to showcase his art collection, just as Hearst had done a century before. His architects, Jane Siris and Peter Coombs, have considerable experience of penthouse conversion and living. Their proposals, which included extensive consultation with New York's Landmarks Preservation Committee, as well as the construction of a 1/16-scale balsa wood model, involved the creation of two new elements to support the refurbished mansard. New windows were added to the structure, which is now a vast living room decorated with the client's collection of Art Deco, Art Nouveau and Arts and Crafts architectural elements.

Unlike many classic penthouse structures, Clarendon Penthouse stands alone, its views across the Hudson River unobstructed and with little overlooking from nearby apartments. New additions include a solarium, guest bedroom and a study, adding 650 square metres (7,000 square feet) of internal space, and externally an additional 929 square metres (10,000 square feet) of terracing, planted with mature trees and shrubs. A terracotta colour has been used on the external walls, further accentuating the feel of a free-standing house surrounded by gardens on top of the city.

Above: **Clarendon Penthouse.** Extremely generous external space, arranged over several levels, characterises the penthouse. The upper level terrace, screened by the trellis shown here, overlooks the Hudson River

Below: Clarendon Penthouse. The penthouse is characterised by its generous ceiling heights, a legacy of Hearst's desire to show off his collection to the full. This west-facing terrace is well planted and screened

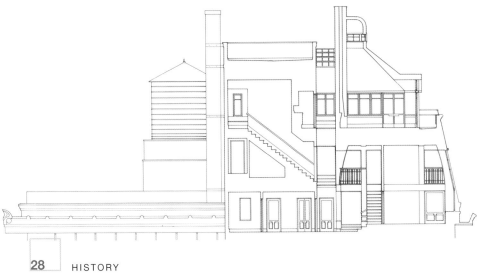

Above: Clarendon Penthouse. A view of the east-facing terrace

Left: Clarendon Penthouse. A section through the refurbished and extended apartment

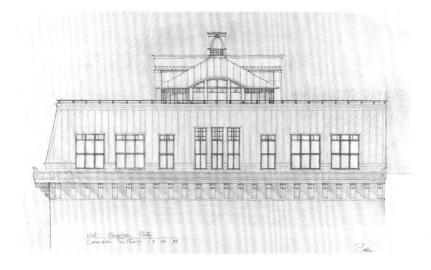

Left: **Clarendon Penthouse.** Elevation showing the generous mansard and former gallery. Their formal appearance disguises the more ad hoc nature of the terraces and services behind them

Below: **Clarendon Penthouse.** A general view from the north-east, showing the penthouse, terraces and river beyond

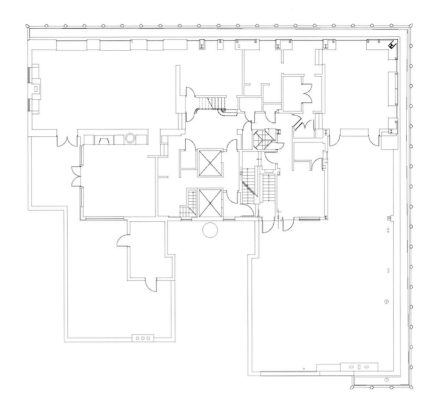

Right: **Clarendon Penthouse.** Plan of the first level of the penthouse

Below: **Clarendon Penthouse.** Looking back at the top-floor pavilion, just one of many external spaces carved from the original, extraordinary penthouse

Claridge's Penthouses

Oswald Milne

London 1932

No less lavish than its American cousins, Oswald Milne's Art Deco design penthouse sits atop Claridge's. The famous London hotel opened in its current incarnation in 1898, with a history that stretched back some 86 years and was consolidated by the amalgamation of five terrace houses on Brook Street. The current building was the result of the hotel's acquisition in 1893 by Richard D'Oyly Carte, owner of the Savoy. D'Oyly Carte set about reconstructing the hotel to designs by CW Stephens, incorporating the very latest in building technology, including lifts, electricity and en-suite bathing facilities. An additional block was constructed at the same time.

At the end of the 1920s, after an extensive renovation by Basil Ionides, the architect Oswald Milne was commissioned to redesign the entrance and create an exclusive two-bedroom suite on the seventh floor for D'Oyly Carte's daughter. Described by a contemporary magazine as 'somewhat after the American "pent-house" fashion', the apartment had views south across London, with doors in the the salon opening on to a 'garden terrace' and metal-framed windows set in semicircular bays in true Art Deco style. Milne also designed all the built-in Japanese chestnut furniture, including a writing desk and cocktail cabinet. The layout was extremely simple – two bedrooms located off a grand central salon, with a generous terrazzo-paved terrace planted with its own herbaceous border. There was no kitchen – this was a serviced apartment. Fixtures and fittings used the very latest technology; the bathrooms even had their own telephones. Now renamed the Brook Suite, and extensively restored at the end of the 1990s by David Law, the penthouse is available for anyone to hire, funds permitting.

In constant demand by the world's wealthiest people, yet impervious to any changes in decorative fashion, luxury hotels offer the perfect introduction to the upper echelons of penthouse living. Hugely expensive to hire, immaculately maintained by armies of invisible staff and providing unparalleled views of some of the world's great cities, the hotel penthouse is one of the last survivors of the great age of penthouse design.

Other notable hotel penthouses include the Dorchester's Audley, Harlequin, Oliver Messel and Terrace Roof Garden suites in London, and the recently created Etoile Suite on top of the Meurice, rue de Rivoli, Paris (the city's most expensive hotel room). The Presidential Suite at Hotel Principe di Savoia, Milan, covers the entire 10th floor, 464 square metres (5,000 square feet) of space with three bedrooms, a 30 metre (98 foot) private pool, spa complex and terrace. Even larger is the elegant Art Deco penthouse suite at Hotel Martinez, Cannes, 743 square metres (8,000 square feet). It overlooks the Mediterranean, from 609 square metres (6,550 square feet) of terraces.

Right: Claridge's Penthouses – Brook Penthouse. The refurbished interior of Milne's Claridge's penthouse, originally designed as a residence for Miss D'Oyly Carte and known as the Brook Penthouse

Below: Claridge's Penthouses – Davies Penthouse. Milne's work was largely the cosmetic enhancement of the upper floors of CW Stephen's hotel, itself refurbished by the Art Deco stylist Basil Ionides in the 1920s

Below: Claridge's Penthouses – Davies Penthouse. The Davies Penthouse is the more traditional of the hotel's two best suites. Each comes with a personal butler for the duration of your stay

Above left: Claridge's Penthouses – Davies Penthouse. The marbled entrance lobby of the hotel's traditionally-styled Davies Penthouse.

Above right: Claridge's Penthouses – Brook Penthouse. The Brook Penthouse retains much of the original 1930s fittings, including this lavish marble bathroom suite

Above: **Claridge's Penthouses.** The internal hallway illustrates the generous circulation space allocated by the designers, giving the apartment more in common with its contemporaries in New York than with anything in London

Right: **Claridge's Penthouses – Brook Penthouse.** The circular bay, a classic Art Deco feature, retains its formal elegance

Left and below: Claridge's Penthouses – Davies Penthouse. Restored and refurbished to extremely high standards, as befits one of London's most expensive hotel rooms, the Davies Penthouse has two bedrooms and approximately 220 square metres (2,368 square feet) of accommodation. The sitting room, shown here, retains its original barrel-vaulted ceiling and generous metal-framed windows overlooking the city

Above: **Claridge's Penthouses – Davies
Penthouse.** The Davies Penthouse is one of the
few spaces in London that equates with the
combination of new money and old world charm
so effortlessly generated by the rooftop mansions
along Fifth Avenue. Restored in the finest tradition
of contemporary interior design, period furniture is
matched with peerless service; guests would
expect nothing less

The Modernist Penthouse

The provision of a roof terrace was one of Le Corbusier's Five Points of Architecture, and the architect exploited light and views wherever possible – he kept a home and studio on the top floor of his apartment building at Porte Molitor in Paris, finished in 1933. It's perhaps no coincidence that many of the architects who advocated the new high-rise, super-dense housing unit spawned by Modernism lived in high-rise apartments themselves, although the two worlds often had little in common. The difference between the Modernist penthouse and the high-rise flat is striking, not least in the way in which the 'vertical street' arrangement of the typical flat engenders claustrophobia and a lack of privacy, two factors entirely absent from the penthouse with its sprawling horizons and private views.

For Corbusier, the roof terrace was an essential, be it sun decks at the small suburban houses in Pessac, larger dwellings like the Maison La Roche (1923) and the Villa Savoye (1928), or terraces at larger apartment buildings like the Immeuble le Ciarté in Geneva (1930). Most famously of all, the Unité d'Habitation in Marseilles featured a rooftop nursery, pool and sun deck, a manmade landscape running the length of the vast building, echoing the

The Modernist Penthouse

mountains surrounding the city. Corbusier described these spaces as *solariums*, well aware of contemporary medical research which highlighted the sun's beneficial and medicinal properties. It was the age of the vogueish suntan, its popularity anecdotally attributed to a 1923 incident in which the fashion designer Coco Chanel appeared bronzed and dark in public, after allegedly having accidentally overindulged in the ultraviolet while on a yachting holiday.

In America, too, advocates of the new architecture were promoting the terrace as a source of health and vitality. Richard Neutra's Lovell Health House in Los Angeles (1928), with its outdoor exercise areas, was set into a steep California hillside so the entrance was effectively at the top floor, turning the entire house into a terrace from which one descended into the glass-swathed, concrete-framed interior. External sleeping decks were a common feature of Modern Movement houses. The Modernists promoted the terrace as a necessity, not a luxury, a simple expedient for making the most of available space, especially in dense urban areas where a garden might not be possible. Any lingering elitism was initially absent; these were democratic rooftop spaces, far removed from the colonnaded, Neo-classical and pseudo-Baroque terraces that sat out of reach atop the Fifth Avenue ziggurats.

Regardless of intention, though, the best views were commandeered by

Opposite: **Paris Apartment.** Guard Tillman Pollock Limited, converted an existing janitor's shack into this tiny one-bedroom, rooftop apartment (1994), transforming a humble, leaking structure into a sleek *pied-à-terre* above the city

Left and below: **Kleiser Penthouse.** Two views of
a classic pavilion atop a terrace, designed by the late
Los Angeles architect Harry Stein

the rich, or by canny architects able to give themselves a prime spot. Berthold Lubetkin famously kept a penthouse apartment atop Highpoint Two, the second of his firm Tecton's cutting-edge Modernist dwellings in north London. Equipped with servants' quarters and staircases integrated into the floor plan, Lubetkin's realm in north London was considerably more spacious than the already upscale apartments below. FRS Yorke, author of *The Modern House*, and founding partner of YRM, apparently insisted that the firm's offices incorporate a penthouse apartment, a useful 'above the shop' retreat for the architect intent on creating an image of non-stop work.[1] In the 1930s, Corbusier himself had designed a penthouse on the Champs-Elysées for Charles de Beistégui, a far more upmarket experiment where, according to author Alexander Tzonis, the architect strove to create 'the sensation of a liner in the ocean'.[2] The design blurred the sense of being in the heart of the city, eliding a boundary of elaborately shaped topiary, broad walls of glass and Surrealist touches like a periscope and a wall-mounted classically styled fireplace adjoining the lawn on the upper terrace, the Arc de Triomphe providing an even more formal backdrop.

Just as the social inclusiveness that characterised the International Style was gradually subsumed under the demands of big business and big architecture, so the Modernist penthouse slowly departed from democratic dreams of space, height and views for all. Initially, the new penthouses might have appeared different from the grand staterooms and colonnaded terraces of the apartment blocks and hotels, but their hauteur and luxury were hardly a study in mass-market design. Once again, the unassailable logic of available space takes over: penthouses are a limited commodity and their value will always be high.

Although the new architecture was disdainful of the fussy stepped arrangement of the classically styled high rise, the Modernist penthouse was no less grand. Architects favoured slabs of 20, 30 or 40 storeys that went straight up, without a bend, kink or indent. The terrace was banished and rooftops were reclaimed, this time by the clunky machinery that keeps modern buildings alive, as well as by the occasional helipad or running track; almost a return to the servile roof spaces of old.

The corporate tower housed a new breed of penthouse dweller, the CEO. Typically, the corporate penthouse was an oversized office suite, following a tradition as old as the flagship skyscrapers of Madison Avenue. Witness the three-storey penthouse, complete with glasshouse, available to Philip Morris executives in their 43-storey, 1931 building at 275 Madison Avenue, or even the mysterious Cloud Club on the 66th, 67th and 68th floors of the Chrysler Building. As the International Style took hold, corporate penthouses owed their design increasingly to high-rise clubs, bars and restaurants rather than to homes; they were slick venues given over to art collections, expensive furniture and acres of space, all transparent symbols of a company's wealth and status. Meeting rooms and lobbies were supported by lounges and even

Opposite: **Show Apartment.** Designed in 2002 by the London-based Czech architect Eva Jiricna, this sumptuously detailed and furnished three-bedroom apartment at the Berkeley Tower development in London's Canary Wharf showcases the ideal Modernist lifestyle

Paul Rudolph Apartment   New York

This New York triplex was home to the late architect Paul Rudolph. Starting in the 1960s, Rudolph used the Beekman Place apartment as a technological sounding board, a space to experiment with spatial arrangements and new materials. The original 19th-century building has been completely reinterpreted along Constructivist lines. Although it is billed as a triplex, there are actually around 30 distinct levels in the space, which has a disorienting array of reflective and transparent surfaces. At the summit, glass additions seem to burst from the original building, a contemporary accretion that is part pavilion, part alien spacecraft. For the most part, Rudolph, who died in 1997, omitted such conventional niceties as balconies, handrails and landings, and walkways are made of glass, ensuring dizzying views up and down through the space (a sensation exacerbated by a contemporary furniture collection that included transparent seats and tables). This makes the penthouse unique, a historic site yet also a functioning, albeit unusual family home.

Top and above: **Albion Riverside.** A new addition (2004) to London's stock of Thames-side apartment buildings. Designed by Foster & Partners, the curvaceous structure includes several generous penthouses

sleeping quarters for time-zone-dazed CEOs and their extensive staff. The tradition continues, from Christian de Portzamparc's 23-storey tower for the luxury goods group LVMH (opened in 1999), with its upper floor function space devoted to fashion parties and launches, to the peak of the dome at 30 St Mary's Axe in London, Norman Foster and Ken Shuttleworth's reworking of the skyscraper form, where a private dining room is made available for the building's tenants.

The Modernist fascination with the juxtaposition of inside and outside spaces has yet to abate. Perhaps more than anything in nature, the urban skyline provides the most seductive landscape with which to integrate, something that Hollywood set-builders have understood for decades. For the Modernist architect obsessed with light and views, the terrace could almost be seen as superfluous, given the possibilities of glass as a means of placing oneself within the city. Nonetheless, fresh air symbolised health and vitality.

Without a terrace, the penthouse would be just another apartment. The crucial difference was in the planning and arrangement of internal spaces. While the great apartment builders of the interwar period took their inspiration from a formal classical approach, the Modernist penthouse was more free-form. In New York in particular, where real estate is marketed in terms of number of rooms, free-form Modernist planning was at odds with the endless round of salons, dining rooms, suites, studies, living rooms and kitchens that made up the traditional apartment. Modernist planning placed the emphasis on free-flowing space – hence the desire for large, inside–outside melding windows. Whether it was a design for a high rise or a lakeside pavilion, open plan was *de rigueur*.

It's tempting to draw a parallel between the rise of the open-plan apartment and the essentially closed and restrictive nature of the International Style facade. Sleek glass and steel facades might have seemed the antithesis of the penthouse ideal, but they gave free rein to fantasies of the interior. Inside, the new penthouses were miniature skylines, internal landscapes played out in double, even treble height spaces, film sets against which the wealthy could play out their lifestyles, displaying extensive art and furniture collections in spaces that imitated the grandeur of a public museum. Elements like internal staircases and private elevators served to detach the experience of the penthouse from the tower upon which it sat; separate, private circulation routes. Even though the floor-to-ceiling glass walls of the new architecture did not open, being on high was still a powerful draw.

Notes
1 Jeremy Melvin, *FRS Yorke and the Evolution of English Modernism*, Wiley-Academy (London), 2003.
2 Alexander Tzonis, *Le Corbusier: The Poetics of Machine and Metaphor*, Thames and Hudson (London), 2001, p 123.

Above: São Paulo Cityscape. High rise and low rise, rich and poor, collide in the modern city

Highpoint Two

Berthold Lubetkin

London 1936–8

One of the first modern European penthouses, and certainly the first in Britain, Berthold Lubetkin's Highpoint Two penthouse was the crowning glory of the Russian-born architect's controversial north London apartment building. Highpoint Two rose alongside its higher sister, Highpoint One, from 1936 to 1938. Highpoint Two and followed the hugely praised Highpoint one a Corbusian vision in white atop one of London's most prominent pieces of high land. Despite critical acclaim, local groups were outraged at the alien form of the new structure, with its projecting balconies, strips of metal windows and soaring canopies.

Highpoint Two therefore had to be different from its predecessor. For a start, the site was more expensive, and fewer flats were allowed, raising the quality in order to make the development work. The central part of the new block, which eschewed Highpoint One's cross-shaped floor plan in favour of a single slab block, contained maisonette apartments with up to four bedrooms. Maids' rooms were on the ground floor, with a service elevator rising discreetly up each wing. The floor plan was further subdivided into two systems of circulation, one for residents, the other for services and tradesmen. As John Allan noted in his comprehensive work on Lubetkin, 'at Highpoint Two, servants could be summoned and despatched discreetly without ever trespassing on their employers' prestige spaces'.[1]

Lubetkin designed the penthouse for his own use, inspired in part by Le Corbusier's 1933 Parisian penthouse. Filled with chunky home-made furniture and quirky touches such as shelves lining the edges of the rooms on which Surrealist *objets trouvés* could rest, and overlooking the tree tops below, the Highpoint Two penthouse was a uniquely personal space. The main living area sat beneath a blue-painted high vaulted roof carefully formed from a thin shell of prefabricated concrete. Custom-built cabinets housed Lubetkin's collection of huge antique volumes, while the furniture and wall coverings were esoteric, to say the least. Upon completion in 1938, the apartment, which occupied about half of the roof area of the block, was the highest in London. From the dining room one looked out over Hampstead Heath through a finely glazed, 7.6 metre (25 foot) long window.

Clearly, this was no ascetic Modernist space to which the architect could retreat for contemplation. Like the earlier Lawn Road Flats, another iconic north London Modernist housing project, Highpoint became a focal point of the burgeoning Modernist social scene. The apartment was the forerunner of the Modernist penthouse, a structure that appeared to sit lightly on its host

Above: **Highpoint Two.** Looking out of the living room across Highgate towards London, Lubetkin's penthouse introduced a new perspective on the city

Above: **Highpoint Two.** The living room was characterised by its barrel-vaulted ceiling, originally painted sky blue. Lubetkin's often rigorous architectural approach belied an eclectic personal taste, evinced by chunky, hand-made furniture (since lost and recreated) and decorative touches like the single panel of wallpaper

building, the delicacy of the connection made all the more emphatic by the extensive use of glass, open-plan living spaces and the dissolve between the inside and outside. The eclecticism of the decor was also contrary to Modernism's perceived austerity – '[the apartment] represents a break away from the hardness and untouchability that has often seemed inevitable in modern interiors,' as Allan quotes from the *Architectural Review*.

Was it a contradiction in terms to be a penthouse-dwelling socialist architect? Perhaps. It was certainly ahead of its time. The Lubetkins' casual furniture, hewn from Norwegian yew by the architect and his wife and covered with Argentinean cow hide, were the prototypes for a million oversized contemporary pieces, designed to make an impact in the increasingly over-scaled modern loft. Like so much of the architecture from this era, the Highpoint Two penthouse fell into disrepair, its most striking features either removed or covered over. A lengthy restoration under the supervision of Allan, now the foremost conservator of Modernist-era buildings in the UK, brought the penthouse back to its former glory in 1996.

Note

1   John Allan, *Berthold Lubetkin: Architecture and the Tradition of Progress*, RIBA Publications (London), 1992, p 293.
2   John Allan, 'The Penthouse', *Architectural Review* Supplement, July 1939, pp 41–50.

Above: **Highpoint Two.** The penthouse's barrel-vaulted ceiling brought a classical vocabulary of form into a Modernist context, an example of Lubetkin's playful approach

Left: **Highpoint Two.** The wide window sills doubled as display cases for Lubetkin's own eclectic selection of objects, or, as seen here, as extensions of the seating in the living area

Keeling House Penthouse

Munkenbeck + Marshall Architects

London 1957, refurbished 1999–2001

Completed in 1957, Denys Lasdun's Keeling House was once considered one of the most architecturally advanced tower blocks in London. This vertical 'street in the sky' rose above the cramped neighbouring terraces as a very visible symbol of Modernism's desire to provide a better way of life for all, without compromising the proximity that generated the community spirit integral to its East End location. Four 15-storey wings were arranged off a central spine, each containing two-storey maisonettes. Circulation corridors were external and space was provided for clothes drying and communal meeting points, as in the traditional streetscape.

There is no room in this book to catalogue the issues – be they social or architectural – that led to the tower block being discredited as a means of mass housing. Suffice to say that, regardless of critical accolades, Keeling House eventually became surplus to requirements and its tenants were rehoused elsewhere. In 2001, the block was overhauled by a residential developer to create 64 duplex and triplex apartments.

The London architectural firm of Munkenbeck + Marshall was charged with refurbishing the structure, bringing it up to date and maximising its potential as a modern, desirable place to live. The site was fenced off, removing the ground level interaction with the street and the surrounding housing, a new entrance lobby was added, with new landscaping and a reflecting pool outside. The uppermost apartments have external terraces and wide-ranging views, but were not treated as penthouses as such – rather, they are 'terrace apartments', their living rooms placed at the top of the three storeys with bedrooms at the bottom.

Driven by the need to make the very most of the building's potential, the decision was taken to create a new penthouse space at the very top of the building, reusing a former water tank made redundant by the addition of decentralised services during refurbishment. The idea was controversial, not least because it involved alterations to a major – and listed – work of postwar architecture. Yet the proposed use of prefabricated parts to speed

Above: **Keeling House Penthouse.** Keeling House seen from an adjoining traditional terraced street. The tower, completed in 1957, was intended to be a vertical 'street in the sky'

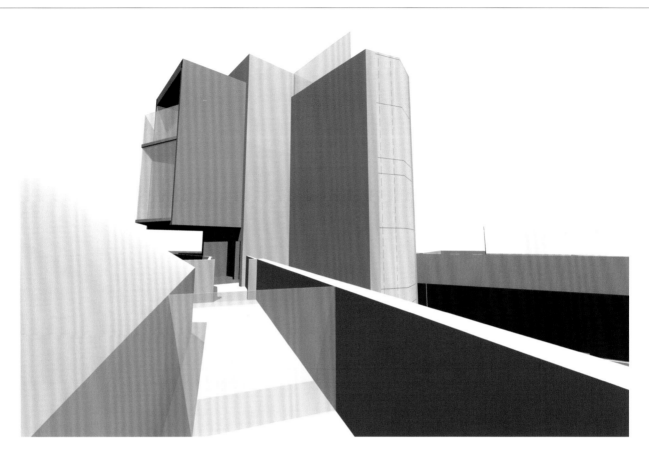

construction, and the fact that the revisions were approved by Lasdun himself before his death in 2001, ultimately won the authorities over. The three-storey penthouse is compact but carefully planned, a continuation of the building's central service spine. At the side, angled louvred glass panels obviate concerns about privacy and overlooking by existing flats, while the stair tower is raised to lead to a private roof terrace right at the summit of the building.

In cramped urban centres, there has recently been a vogue for converting the original wave of tower blocks into private rather than social housing. Few schemes achieve a solution as elegant as that of Munkenbeck + Marshall, preferring instead to overclad the original structure to hide its functional origins.

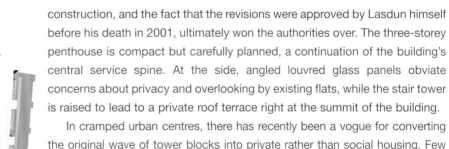

Above: **Keeling House Penthouse.** Computer-generated image of the new penthouse element, a modest structure that occupies vacant space around the central spine of the building

Left: **Keeling House Penthouse.** Computer-generated image of the refurbished building, illustrating how the new penthouse continues the line of the central spine

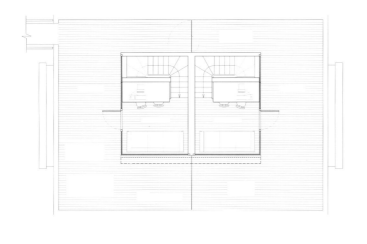

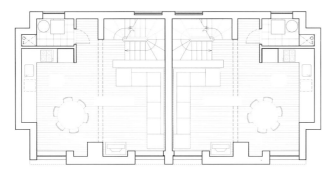

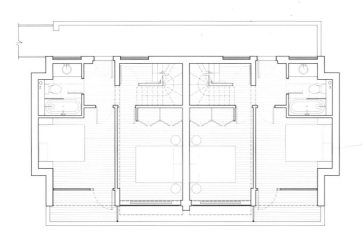

From top: **Keeling House Penthouse.** Proposed
roof terrace and terrace room; proposed upper-floor
plan; proposed lower-floor plan

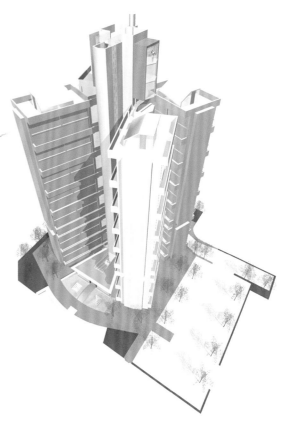

Above: **Keeling House Penthouse.** Computer-
generated aerial view

Below: **Keeling House Penthouse.** Computer-generated aerial view

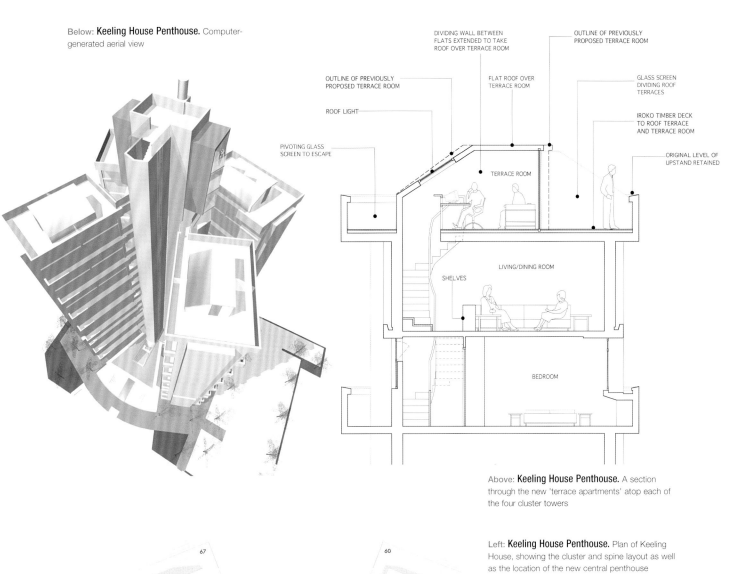

DIVIDING WALL BETWEEN
FLATS EXTENDED TO TAKE
ROOF OVER TERRACE ROOM

OUTLINE OF PREVIOUSLY
PROPOSED TERRACE ROOM

OUTLINE OF PREVIOUSLY
PROPOSED TERRACE ROOM

FLAT ROOF OVER
TERRACE ROOM

GLASS SCREEN
DIVIDING ROOF
TERRACES

ROOF LIGHT

IROKO TIMBER DECK
TO ROOF TERRACE
AND TERRACE ROOM

PIVOTING GLASS
SCREEN TO ESCAPE

ORIGINAL LEVEL OF
UPSTAND RETAINED

TERRACE ROOM

LIVING/DINING ROOM

SHELVES

BEDROOM

Above: **Keeling House Penthouse.** A section through the new 'terrace apartments' atop each of the four cluster towers

Left: **Keeling House Penthouse.** Plan of Keeling House, showing the cluster and spine layout as well as the location of the new central penthouse

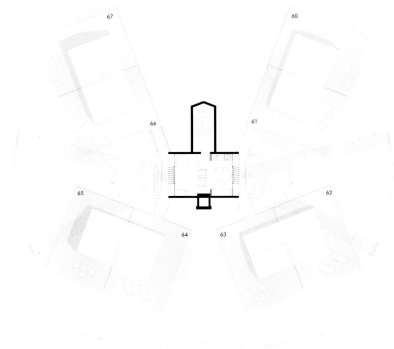

The Playboy Penthouse

Humen Tan

Published in Playboy, September 1956

Few publications were as explicit as *Playboy* in drawing parallels between the more eccentric and expressive tendencies of modern design and the emerging consumer lifestyle. In September 1956, the magazine embarked on the first of four architectural fantasies, employing the Chicago-based architectural draughtsman Humen Tan to encapsulate the periodical's editorial ethos in physical form.

The result were *Playboy*'s Penthouse Apartment, which debuted that month, followed by *Playboy*'s Weekend Hideway (April 1959), The Playboy Town House (May 1962) and, finally, *Playboy*'s Patio-Terrace (August 1963). All four epitomised Hugh Hefner's passionate marriage of consumption, pleasure and, most important of all, an urban-based lifestyle. Not for *Playboy* an audience from the massed ranks of tract housing, however stylish, that were multiplying across post-Levittown America. Instead, *Playboy* targeted the urbanist reader, the contemporary flâneur who enjoyed the finer things in life.

The *Playboy* series of architectural projects placed a remarkably prescient emphasis on in-home technology (the penthouse apartment featured an 'electronic entertainment wall' with hi-fi, AM–FM radio, television and space for 2,000 LPs). There were even individual furniture projects, such as the *Playboy* Rotating Bed, showcased in the issue for November 1959 and apparently popular with do-it-yourself inclined readers.

The penthouse came first, 'a high, handsome haven – pre-planned and furnished for the bachelor in town'. The urban location, clean lines and generally modern, forward-looking aspect of the apartment are emphasised at every step. The magazine is under no illusion; this is a space for a bachelor to hold court and stage-manage frequent romantic rendezvous: it is as far removed from mass-market domesticity as the great Fifth Avenue penthouses were from the homes of the average American. Yet the principal difference is not one of location and aspect but of aspiration – this was the penthouse as a consumerist palace, bringing together high and low culture, mixing pop and classics, the home of a true connoisseur. *Playboy*'s penthouse was a Modernist structure, with a futuristic kitchen reminiscent of the one in Alison and Peter Smithson's House of the Future (exhibited the same year), furniture designed by the likes of Saarinen and Herman Miller, art by Willem de Kooning and reconfigurable walls using sliding Japanese-style shoji screens.

While strong parallels may be drawn with the Californian Case Study House programme, then in full swing, the crucial difference was that Art and Architecture's epoch-defining residential designs were for detached houses

Below: **The Playboy Penthouse Apartment.** The open-plan layout of the penthouse. Kitchen space is kept to a minimum; this is an apartment for entertaining and leisure, not traditional domesticity

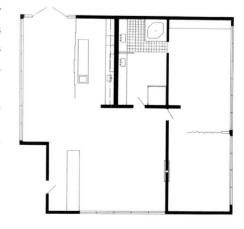

'PLAYBOY PENTHOUSE APARTMENT' PLAYBOY MAGAZINE (SEPTEMBER 1956, PP 54–5). ARTIST: HUMEN TAN

Above: The Playboy Penthouse Apartment. The penthouse in all its glory: 'More than a place to hang his hat, a man dreams of his own domain, a place that is exclusively his.'

occupying virgin sites, not city centre locations. *Playboy*'s town house, designed by the architect R Donald Jaye, was described as 'posh plans for exciting urban living' and eschewed suburbia in favour of a distinctly urban, terraced site. Provision was made for servants' quarters in the basement (along with a glass-walled pool and a carport, shown containing a rakish E-type Jaguar). Full-height floor-to-ceiling glazing in the living area imported the very latest in architectural design.

Finally, *Playboy*'s patio-terrace, a generous 396 square metres (4,260 square feet) that included a pool and raised cantilevered sun deck (to permit 'terrace activities of a less-sedentary nature to go on unimpeded'), comprised the latest in design and technology, including Bertoia chairs, surround-sound

'The Playboy Town House' Playboy magazine (May 1962, p 83). Artist: Humen Tan

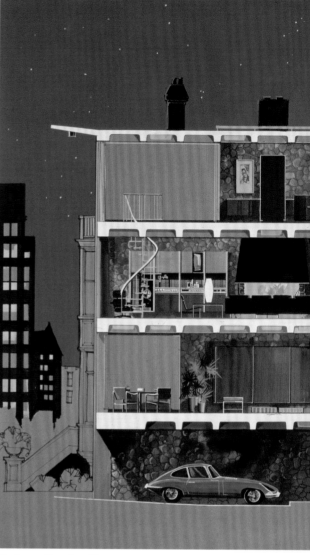

'The Playboy Town House' Playboy magazine (May 1962, pp 84–5). Artist: Humen Tan

Above left and right: The Playboy Town House.
Two views of 1962's *Playboy* town house, an elegant Modernist confection that shrugs off any hint of suburbia. Complete with roof terrace, covered pool and, again, ample entertaining space, this was presented to readers as the ultimate town house

speakers and an external kitchen. Described as 'an urban oasis which delightfully avoids the crawl through country-bound traffic', the terrace was designed to adjoin a penthouse as an 'island in the metropolitan sun'.

Although the *Playboy* projects placed more emphasis on technology and furnishings than on architectural styling, these urban projects signal the post-war shift in taste towards penthouse living as traditional modes of domestic accommodation began to aspire to Modernism's more attractive elements – space, light and technology – and the old-school penthouse faded from memory. *Playboy*'s readers devoured the schemes. The magazine reported that many went as far as constructing their own versions of the stylised plans, with designs such as the round bed proving especially popular. Naturally, it was modelled on the original bed, housed in the fabled mansion. For all the talk of modern living, for the ultimate playboy nothing short of baronial comfort would do.

'THE PLAYBOY TOWN HOUSE' PLAYBOY MAGAZINE (MAY 1962, PP 86–7). ARTIST: HUMEN TAN

'PLAYBOY PENTHOUSE APARTMENT' PLAYBOY MAGAZINE (SEPTEMBER 1956, P 57). ARTIST: HUMEN TAN

Above: **The Playboy Penthouse Apartment.**
Furnishings and fittings are relentlessly
contemporary: 'A Saarinen couch and the classic
Saarinen armchair with Versen floor lamp complete
a charmed circle'

Right: **Playboy's Patio Terrace.** This presented a
veritable rooftop playroom, a composition of pool,
loungers, planters and an extensive outdoor barbecue
kitchen, greening up *Playboy* man's lifestyle

Opposite: **The Playboy Town House.** The rotating
circular bed was a popular *Playboy* device that was
first featured in the magazine in 1959. The
suggested decor has more in common with an
upscale office than a domestic space, with an
emphasis on gadgets and technology

'PLAYBOY'S PATIO TERRACE' PLAYBOY MAGAZINE (AUGUST 1963, P 96–7). ARTIST: HUMEN TAN

Above: **Playboy's Patio Terrace.** The magazine described the patio-terrace as an 'island in the metropolitan sun' and saw it as a way of humanising the city. 'No cosmopolite is immune to an occasional longing for some parcel of sky-domed greensward to offset the concrete, chrome, glass and steel that may make city living elegant and convenient – but decidedly non-pastoral.'

'PLAYBOY'S PATIO TERRACE' PLAYBOY MAGAZINE (AUGUST 1963, PP 98–9). ARTIST: HUMEN TAN

The Deck House

John Young/Richard Rogers Partnership
London 1986–9

This riverside penthouse has become one of the icons of High-tech architecture. Designed by the architect John Young, who still occupies the apartment, it was built as part of a new housing development that lies adjacent to the Thames-side offices of the Richard Rogers Partnership, where Young is a long-standing partner.

The Deck House is a sustained expression of the way technology can be transposed into residential architecture, using numerous elements, materials, methods and processes developed for industrial buildings. In this respect, it draws intellectual and aesthetic inspiration from Pierre Chareau's Maison de Verre in Paris (completed in 1932), paradoxically a house located in a tight urban site rather than on a London rooftop. While Chareau used a curtain wall of glass blocks in place of a conventional wall, ostensibly to bring light into the house, Young recreates this visual feat with the dramatic circular shower tower on the roof of the Deck House, a gesture with stylistic rather than purely functional overtones.

Like Chareau, Young has utilised industrial components for ventilation, shelving and partitioning, adapting them for his own purposes. The Deck House demonstrates a singular commitment to technical perfection, its many key elements custom-built by industries usually considered to be outside of the domestic sphere, such as shopfitters and boat-builders. The finished look fetishises industrial components: stacked circular wall-mounted radiators, gleaming stainless-steel extractor pipes, a complex staircase-cum-gangplank and library-issue shelving overclad in brushed stainless steel and operated with yacht-style wheels.

Upstairs, the circular, glass brick shower room is topped by an observation deck, reached by a finely engineered spiral staircase that winds around it. The architect's desire to maximise the visual drama of elevated outdoor spaces is directly linked to the classic penthouse tradition.

Opposite: **The Deck House.** The penthouse is topped by this remarkable circular bathroom, a temple to bathing constructed from glass bricks and industrial elements which are transferred into the domestic realm. Here, the penthouse aesthetic returns to its preresidential origins, as plant room and machinery atop the structure, albeit machinery for maintaining humans, not buildings

Opposite: **The Deck House.** The penthouse is the principal element in the Richard Rogers Partnership's Thames Reach development, which has a quasi-industrial/nautical theme. Great expanses of glass are set off against carefully calibrated high-tech components, such as the wall-mounted circular radiators and the complex staircase

Above: **The Deck House.** Seen from the adjacent Victorian-scale residential street, the Deck House presents itself as an almost alien object, its residential function not necessarily obvious

Left: **The Deck House.** The dual-aspect character of this end-of-terrace block gives fantastic views from within the apartment, as well as from the deck above

Glen Street Penthouse

Harry Seidler and Associates

Sydney 1989

Glen Street is home to Harry Seidler's office, a purpose-built six-storey structure designed by the architect in the early 1970s. The building was always a strong architectural statement, its windows set back behind a gridded facade of angled concrete louvres. In the late 1980s, the firm constructed an addition adjacent to the original office, expanding the commercial floor space and creating a dramatic Modernist penthouse at its peak. The new building uses the same visual language as its precursor but has a less formal plan owing to site constraints. The beautifully shuttered concrete panels bend to create a curve in the facade just above the new entrance, which is indicated by its canopy, formed from one of Seidler's trademark grand-piano curves.

The new penthouse occupies the fifth and sixth floors of the building. Accessed independently using the same stair core as the office, it is also used by the business, having been designed specifically with the nature of architectural practice in mind. A small theatre/presentation space is incorporated and shared with the office. The penthouse's double-height reception area, dominated by the sweep of the staircase up to the mezzanine, also functions as a space for receptions.

The blank canvas afforded by the integration of the penthouse into the construction of a whole new six-storey block, and its status as the only residential element of the design, allowed Seidler free rein to emphasise the dramatic views from the sweep of windows on the west elevation. The set-back west facade runs in a continuous curve, opening out on to a terrace that bulges slightly in the centre of the apartment to accommodate external seating, with a dramatic view of Sydney Harbour Bridge.

Inside, the attention to detail focuses on the view; the dining table is a half ellipse and is positioned so that guests face the views and the hosts face them on the other side. The sixth floor is given over to the master suite, study and seating area. Seidler's extensive collection of postwar art adorns the walls, while the furnishings, in the original scheme at least, are Modernist classics by Le Corbusier and Marcel Breuer, their monochrome metal and black leather in no way detracting from the colourful artworks and larger sculptural elements like the balcony and stair.

Seidler's residential work frequently encompasses high rises, most notably the 1990 Horizon Apartments in Sydney. This 43-storey tower features generous 'wave'-shaped balconies which curve outwards from the facade to create a distinctive finned effect. The top two storeys contain penthouses, with balconies oriented towards the Pacific, to better exploit the high vantage point.

Right: Glen Street Penthouse. Careful consideration was given to framing views across and through the various zones in the apartment. From here, on the mezzanine, the eye is drawn to a solitary Le Corbusier recliner, actually in the corner of the master bedroom. Directly below it can be seen the back row of seats in the private theatre used for client presentations

Below: Glen Street Penthouse. The lower floor of the penthouse level. The balcony beyond overlooks Sydney Harbour

Right: **Glen Street Penthouse.** The external facade of the original Glen Street building, with its distinctive grid of concrete window sunscreens. The penthouse was added to the structure in 1989, 16 years after it was originally completed

Below: **Glen Street Penthouse.** Looking from penthouse mezzanine level, where the bedrooms are located. Great organic curves on the mezzanine balustrade echo the building's curving facade

Above: **Glen Street Penthouse.** The curved forms are
at their most exaggerated in the balustrade of the spiral
stair, framing the Frank Stella sculpture on the wall

Above: Glen Street Penthouse. Looking across to the upper floor lounge. The dining table, seen below, was designed as a half ellipse, allowing all the guests to sit on the curved edge with the view of the harbour, while the hosts face them on the straight edge

Right: Glen Street Penthouse. Just one of several sitting areas. The chairs throughout the penthouse are designed by Marcel Breuer

Below: **Glen Street Penthouse.** Another view of
the dining table, this time giving a guest's-eye view
of Sydney Harbour

The Loft and the Contemporary Penthouse

High-level living couldn't last. The penthouses of the golden era were superseded by architectural developments, as the fashion for glass and steel swept across cities, abolishing craggy terraces and exuberant detailing in favour of slab sides and clipped tops. There was now no place for the moneyed urbanist to perch. Meanwhile, modern architecture was also restructuring the city in other ways. As more and more buildings became redundant, city dwellers who needed space, and lots of it, gradually turned to the original, pre-penthouse industrial structures, with New York, once again, leading the way.

Loft living was insular, the hermetically sealed antithesis of penthouse glamour. As the early history of lofts makes clear, the initial trend towards using former industrial locations as living space was not perceived as especially fashionable or glamorous. Instead, it was often a case of economic necessity. Lofts were large, light-filled, centrally located spaces, perfect for postwar artistic practice that was dependent on a critical and intellectual network centred around the East Coast.

New York-based artists such as Robert Rauschenberg, Gerhard Lieber and James Rosenquist practically commandeered old lofts as studios,

The Loft and the Contemporary Penthouse

working and camping in the vast open spaces. Gradually, the ramshackle living arrangements of these pioneering artists found their way into colour supplements and interiors magazines, and more and more creative types jumped on the loft bandwagon.[1]

The loft offered a seductive combination of light and space, an atelier for modern times, drawing succour and inspiration from its industrial origins. Large windows not only let in precious light but framed dramatic urban views (if not the heavenly vistas offered by the penthouse and the terrace and fetishised by Hollywood). As lofts evolved from bohemian beginnings into highly fashionable living spaces – blank canvases for architectural experimentation – the traditional penthouse faded into obscurity. The Fifth Avenue mansions in the sky were still occupied, the doormen still tugged their white gloves on tight and guarded the grand entrances. But even if the marble bathrooms were kept polished and the terraces swept clean, the grand salons and ballrooms had long been subdivided into smaller units as an era passed away.

The loft redefined the way habitable space was created, packaged and marketed in inner cities around the world. But while massive spaces required inventive design to make them habitable, tight economic conditions once again prevailed to spur on innovation. Space remained at a premium. Sites on the ground were either nonexistent or prohibitively expensive, so developers

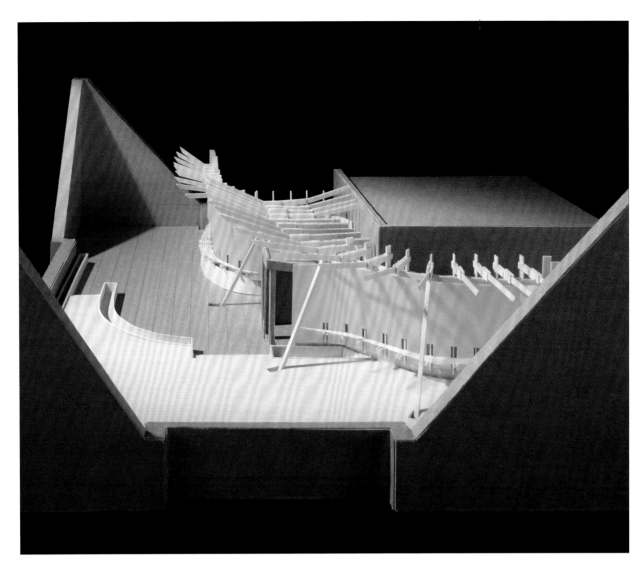

Roof Terrace   Graftworks   New York, 1999

This roof garden is on the 32nd storey of a New York apartment building. Designed to capture views of the East River and midtown Manhattan, the curved, wooden screen also shields the terrace from mechanical equipment. The roof terrace is architectural in its approach, integrating elements such as bench seating, an external basin and shelving to create a room in the sky. The wood is cedar, fashioned into elegant curves using techniques usually found in boat construction. The spiky trellis that crowns the garden is built from steel and wood hybrid beams for wider spans, and is designed to mimic the flight pattern of migratory birds. The design was undertaken by Graftworks, established by Lawrence Blough and John Henle in 1999.

Roof Terrace Graftworks New York, 1999

Roof Terrace Graftworks New York, 1999

A development of 7 live/work units, 3 office units, 18 one, two and three bedroom apartments and 3 spectacular penthouses.

BUXTON
Homes

WARNING
PREMISES RADIO LINKED
TO RAPID RESPONSE UNIT
CCS CLARKE
CONSTRUCTION
SECURITY LTD
0870 900 1473

Right: London, 2004. In a city of soaring aspirations and forests of scaffolding from which a new democracy of penthouses is emerging, these are lower and less spectacular than their predecessors, and their developers are more concerned with the bottom line than the skyline

and their architects looked up. The industrial and commercial buildings being converted into apartments didn't have elaborate roofscapes like the upscale, uptown apartments with their mansards, or office blocks with their miniature cityscapes of machinery and equipment. Instead, they had flat roofs, blank canvases upon which new structures could be built.

Initially, the idea that a loft building might be topped by a penthouse apartment was considered laughable, especially when the grace and style of the Fifth Avenue apartment were compared with the rough and ready multi-thousand-square-foot spaces clawed back from industrial service. Converting industrial buildings provided another angle, however, a clean slate upon which a building could be 'crowned'. New penthouse architecture slowly began to detach itself stylistically from the host building, becoming a form of parasitic growth that increasingly bore little architectural resemblance to the structure below.

A new era was beginning, as roofscapes that previously had been literally overlooked revealed themselves as unbuilt land, hidden development potential above the city streets. The architectural integrity of the early, integrated apartment building gave way to a new eclecticism as the penthouse evolved into a villa in the sky.

This new Modernist penthouse was, in a sense, a return to the structure's roots; an isolated pavilion set aloft and architecturally distinct from its surroundings, just like the overlooked shacks and machinery sheds that littered the first roofscapes. The host building receded into the geography of the city, another peak to scale. Besides, the high rise was being democratised around the world by new housing projects and council estates, all of which saw the vertical city as a means of creating more living space out of less land.

Developers understood the economic logic of penthouses well – almost too well. New residential architecture has become increasingly top-heavy, as the upper floors increase in size and prominence, the better to convey their

Roof Terrace Graftworks New York, 1999

Roof Terrace **Graftworks** New York, 1999

expense and prestige. In London, developments such as St George's Wharf in Vauxhall by Broadway Malyan, the Greenwich Millennium Village by Erskine/Lovatt and numerous Docklands schemes by CZWG all focus on the upper floors, making the apartments below appear dominated and overshadowed. In New York, the Porter House Condo building, designed by ShOP, grafts a strictly Modernist penthouse structure on to an existing facade, making no attempt to disguise the join.

While the dedicated development penthouse has shaped architecture from the ground up, a new low-key penthouse aesthetic has evolved, also arising from the conversion of former industrial buildings, and frequently low rise in comparison to the traditional penthouse. These projects transfer the small-scale Modernist residential aesthetic on to the rooftop, adding additional storeys, opening up the space to the sky and generally conveying the sense of a distinct object in a landscape, just as the iconic Modernist 'box' was defiantly free-standing and anti-picturesque. As with the single family house, the architects and engineers designing such 'pavilion penthouses' are free to play with form and structure or simply to exploit previously overlooked space.

Penthouses have always been an economic and not a social phenomenon. The division between conversion and new build produced two very different aesthetics, yet each is driven by its key position in the carefully organised economic system of development. A penthouse (or, more practically, *penthouses*), is an essential component of a speculative residential development. For a scheme to make economic sense, these high-profile, high-value units flagpost it both physically and in terms of marketing material. It is the penthouse that dominates promotional literature, its views, light and space not necessarily reflecting those of the apartments below. As a result, developments have to build more and more penthouses, creating an architecture that is often compromised. The alternative is the bespoke object on the roofscape, an option available only to a select and fortunate few.

As property prices rise in tandem with the premium on space, several architects have taken the idea of the rooftop object and designed concepts and schemes for more affordable, less elitist penthouses. In the future, the roof of the city might just be a space available to all.

Note
1   Sharon Zukin, *Loft Living: Culture and Capital in Urban Change*, Radius (London), 1998, p 58.

Penthouse Apartment

Johannes Saurer Architekt

Thun, Switzerland 2002

Johannes Saurer's modest penthouse in Thun, central Switzerland, occupies a dramatic site alongside the Aare River. The main living space is a part-glazed pavilion, offering sweeping views of the town's 12th-century castle, a riot of pointed turrets and steep roofs. Surrounded by a small terrace, it has a floor of black slate and a minimally detailed kitchen area lit by a single neon tube suspended on wires from the ceiling. Other details are deliberately quasi-industrial, such as the three copper ventilation pipes on the terrace.

Above: **Penthouse Apartment.** Viewed from across the Aare River, the penthouse looks modest, almost industrial

Above: **Penthouse Apartment.** Closer inspection reveals a minimally detailed glass box surrounded by a small terrace. The integration of the copper ventilation pipes into the composition gives the small structure a quasi-machine-like feel

Right: **Penthouse Apartment.** Internally, the penthouse is integrated into the existing structure, with all finishes kept crisp and white

Above: **Penthouse Apartment.** The main living space fulfils the requirement for space, light and views. However, Saurer has deliberately eschewed expensive materials and fittings in favour of details like the single fluorescent tube over the slab-like kitchen units

Treehouse

Block Architecture

London 2002

This urban apartment overlooks Hoxton Square, the nexus of the East End revival in fashion, art and bar culture. Designed by Block Architecture's Graham Wilkinson and Zöe Smith, the new space is located on the top floor of a building with views south and east across Hoxton Square to the City of London.

The floor area is relatively modest; in order to maximise the feeling of space an enclosed layout was eschewed in favour of open-plan space. The architects resolved any privacy issues by creating an internal 'treehouse', a cantilevered wooden box that appears to float in the main living space. Beautifully detailed, clad in wooden slats and dramatically underlit, the treehouse contains the master-bed platform, which can be opened to the living area by means of folding screens.

The kitchen island unit is constructed from the same materials, employing the same grid system of slatted timber. At night, internal fittings make the kitchen and sleeping boxes glow from within, thus acting as lanterns inside the space, a visual effect which is especially eye-catching from the extensive terrace outside. All other surfaces are treated minimally – for instance, the white glass and resin bathroom, carefully screened off, with laboratory fixtures to heighten the sense of clinical perfection.

Treehouse design has undergone something of a revival in recent years with several monographs published on the subject, yet the treehouse is a relatively unfamiliar metaphor for architects of urban penthouses. Block are keen to emphasise the role of the treehouse in childhood, a structure associated with 'early creativity, independence, escapism, solitude, and the first kiss'. It's this romanticised view of a transient architectural space that other architects, designers and occupiers appear to have overlooked. A more common description of a penthouse is as an eyrie, a word resonant with symbolism that manages to associate the penthouse occupier's physical and social position above the city with the perceived power and dynamism of an eagle. The treehouse apartment is charming, modest in scale and devoid of the superfluous connotations of power and status that often accompany other penthouses.

Right: **Treehouse.** The Treehouse's extensive terrace, with views over East End rooftops to the City beyond. The same wooden decking is used throughout, bringing continuity to the space

Left: Treehouse. The bathroom uses fixtures and fittings sourced from laboratory and medical suppliers, making it appear clinical and industrial

Far Left: Treehouse. Detail of master-bed 'box' showing a folding screen

Opposite: **Treehouse.** The kitchen counter is illuminated from within, adding extra depth to the structure. At night, the reflections in the sliding glass walls double the perceived size of the space, creating a miniature skyline that mimics the City beyond

Right and below: **Treehouse.** Views of the cantilevered box in the main living space

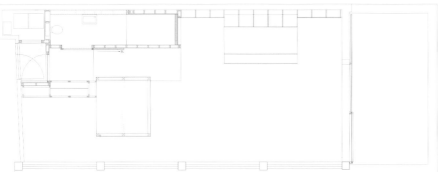

Above: **Treehouse.** The kitchen counter as seen from the entrance. To the left is the box containing the bathroom; to the right is the master-bed 'box'

Left: **Treehouse.** Floor plan of the apartment

Below: **Treehouse.** A slide-out worktop extends
the capacity of the kitchen counter. Tower 42 in the
City of London can be seen in the distance

Mica House Penthouse

Stanton Williams Architects

London 1997

'Intentionally ambiguous' is how the architects describe this space, the conversion of the floor of a former warehouse into a house and office for a private client. Mindful of the restrictions imposed by the traditional home office on a domestic environment, the client asked for a more gallery-like atmosphere, with white walls and stone and wooden floors. The result is an apartment of approximately 230 square metres (2,475 square feet), including an extensive terrace which the L-shaped structure encloses on two sides.

The reductivist approach to the design led to the apartment being pigeon-holed in the nascent Minimalist movement in Britain, buoyed by the high-profile retail and residential work of architects like John Pawson and Claudio Silvestrin and receiving a great deal of media attention. A BBC2 documentary, *Bare*, produced as part of the 'Modern Times' series, even included the penthouse as an example of the benefits – and pitfalls – of living in an open-plan, glass-walled space. In an age before ubiquitous reality television and design makeover shows dulled our response to *outré* interiors, the clients and architects featured in *Bare* appeared slightly hesitant and defensive, as if they felt their taste was being mocked by the programme-makers.

The Mica House apartment is planned as one continuous space. The glass walls leave little of the interior to the imagination, and while there is no seamless, step-free merging of inside and out, the L-shaped plan allows views that go outside, then in again. Situated in a predominantly residential area of Islington, several miles north of the City of London, the apartment offers views that are leafier and less urban, with the distant towers of the Barbican the only real clue to the location. There is none of the inter-apartment voyeurism that one has come to expect from cramped urban living conditions; this penthouse has the skyline all to itself.

The client, a graphic design consultant, aspired to the classic white box, removing ornament and details until all that was left were walls without skirtings, flush doors, a continuous floor surface that runs from inside to outside switching from wooden boards to slats, and large floor-to-ceiling swathes of glass. The main area overlooks the terrace, which is large enough to display sculptures and still function as a usable outdoor space. The terrace is the dominant feature of this pavilion in the sky, making it seem open, light and spacious.

Right: **Mica House Penthouse.** Looking back from the deck into the living space. The way in which the penthouse looks out on to this external court is clear. The master sleeping space is to the right of the picture, while the living room has sliding doors that open on to the deck

Below: **Mica House Penthouse.** Architects often speak about blurring the boundaries between inside and outside. Stanton Williams utilised the high vantage point of this new apartment in north London to establish a secluded courtyard in the air

MLC's New Built Lofts

Manhattan Loft Corporation

Bankside Lofts
Summer Street Lofts
Soho Lofts

The Manhattan Loft Corporation spearheaded the loft conversion movement in London. Founded in 1992 by the German-born, American-raised entrepreneur Harry Handelsman, the firm arrived in the city at an inauspicious time – London was in the grip of the worst postwar property recession to date and great tracts of the city lay undeveloped, their future uncertain.

The MLC introduced the concept of shell space into the city, turning former industrial lofts and warehouses into huge empty spaces that were subdivided and sold by the square foot. All that needed to be added was servicing, plus the contact details of a few high-profile architects. Prospective buyers would then organise the 'fit-out' of their space themselves, hiring architects to shape the empty internal space into something highly personal, a tailor-made apartment with elements of the classic, empty loft space.

The MLC represented the first wave of private investment in areas in need of urban renewal, changing the fortunes of down-at-heel districts of the city. The term 'loft living' entered the language, although it was recognised that London's disused commercial infrastructure was very different in scale to the warehouses of New York and Chicago, out of which the original loft movement had arisen.

As loft living became more popular, commercial pressures saw the raw spaces carved up into increasingly smaller – and arguably un-loft-like – units, so the company came to be accused of selling a lifestyle rather than an actual product. In truth, the MLC's units were noticeably more generous in size than those of its imitators. In addition, the company's strong identification with the American model meant that it recognised the value – both commercial and symbolic – of the penthouse apartment when creating new developments. The MLC's new-build lofts, an inherently contradictory term that swiftly became the market standard once the bulk of existing commercial premises had been snapped up by developers, also used the image of the penthouse.

From the MLC's earliest conversions, like the Summer Street Lofts in Clerkenwell, the firm's strategy has been to expand and add extra accommodation at the top of the building. However, these additions differ from the classic penthouse and the Modernist rooftop pavilion in that they are rarely discreet. Instead, the penthouses feature prominently in promotional literature and sales particulars, and started the fashion for selling a development 'top down', with the most exclusive units marketed hard. The Soho Lofts development on Wardour Street, the conversion of a warehouse complex that once housed the Marquee Club, among other things, features penthouse

Above: **Bankside Lofts.** The external spiral staircase at the penthouse apartment, Bankside Lofts. One of the capital's most dramatic private residences, the Bankside penthouse is located on the south bank of the Thames, looking north

Right: **Summer Street Lofts.** The Summer Street Lofts were an early MLC development. The barrel-vaulted penthouse, seen here, was added on to the existing warehouse structure, not only as a means of domesticising the formerly industrial space, but also as a clear signifier of enhanced value and exclusivity

additions that are relatively low-key when the building is viewed from the dense streets. At roof level, it's another story entirely. The penthouses were sold as shells, empty areas beneath a curving zinc roof, with double-height spaces and terraces that featured prominently in the development's brochure.

More recent and more ambitious projects include West India Quay in east London, where the construction of a dedicated residential tower, Eastern Tower, allows for multiple penthouse units, befitting its position in the heart of London's new financial district. Other schemes, such as Fulham Island, have rooftop gardens. The MLC's first new-build project, the Bankside Lofts, featured a curved tower designed by CZWG, its peak stepped to create generous terraces for the upper storeys, culminating in Handelsman's own multiheight penthouse. Shortly after completion, the company placed a vast, Manhattan-style advertising sign on the upper roof terrace, broadcasting the penthouse lifestyle to thousands of passers-by and commuters rattling out of Blackfriars station towards their ordinary homes in the suburbs.

Above: Bankside Lofts. Blackfriars Bridge and station viewed from the terrace at the Bankside Penthouse. This kind of view was once an anomaly in central London, where only offices aspired to such heights

Right: Soho Lofts. The MLC's Soho Lofts development was enhanced by extensive new penthouses, arranged above the former Marquee Club in central London

Opposite: Bankside Lofts. The interior of one of the penthouses at Bankside Lofts, which also features the MLC's trademark barrel-vaulted space. The huge floor plans were a novelty in British interior design, and the initial wave of loft dwellers enhanced and redesigned these spaces in an eclectic, varied fashion, whether Modernism, High-tech or Minimalism

Above left: **Bankside Lofts.** The Bankside Lofts complex culminates in the terracotta-painted circular tower, which spirals up to a series of stepped terraces and apartments on the upper floor, crowned by the multistorey penthouse

Above right: **Soho Lofts.** Looking out across Soho's rooftops from the new shell penthouses above the Soho Lofts development. Walls of glass maximise the views

Above: **Soho Lofts.** An exterior view of the roof terraces which overlook Soho

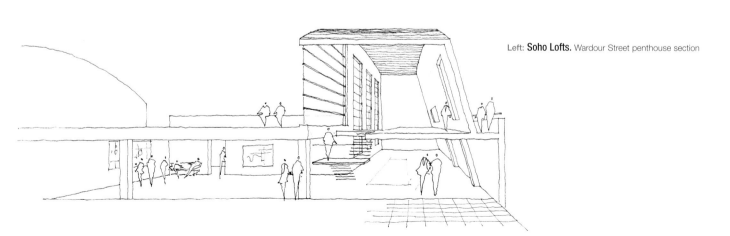

Left: **Soho Lofts.** Wardour Street penthouse section

Penthouse in Manhattan

Tadao Ando Architect & Associates
New York 1999

The Japanese architect Tadao Ando approached the design of a Manhattan penthouse with the intention of creating a unifying object, simultaneously floating above the city it celebrates while complementing the skyline through a deliberately confrontational design. The penthouse was designed to sit at the summit of an existing 1920s skyscraper, formerly the New York headquarters of the London Guarantee & Accident Company, a speculative addition rising above the building's Beaux Arts ornament and elaborate fenestration.

The new structure is composed of three elements: a transparent rectangle formed from a concrete structure wrapped in a skin of glass at the very top, surrounded by a rooftop water garden with a 43 metre long by 6 metre wide (142 x 20 feet) glass box that punches through the original facade five storeys below. This last is of a similar construction to the upper box and houses two bedrooms, a bathroom, kitchen and living area, an inhabited shelf that teeters over the city streets below, bearing no architectural relationship to the existing (and now much altered) floor plan.

The upper box is some 65 metres long (214 feet), aligned with the original building but just overhanging one end. The pool covers half the roof area, placed so as to reflect the cinematic skyline beyond – Ando calls this 'borrowed scenery', a nod to the epic, painted backdrops and model work of early Hollywood, the start of a grand tradition that continues to this day. The building's orginal 'penthouse', in this case an ornate two-storey elevator housing, is transformed into a playful garden pavilion, a rooftop folly adrift in a formally planned Modernist garden. An octagonal 'temple' also stands on the peak, complete with urns and pillars, and this is accommodated within the upper floor glass box.

Ando's proposal, exhibited at the 2002 Venice Architecture Biennale, provided over 697 square metres (7,500 square feet) of space, a penthouse on a truly epic scale, distilling the heterogeneous qualities of New York's 120-year vertical evolution and providing a dramatic platform from which to oversee, assess and experience this most delirious of cities. The emphasis on the horizontal design of the penthouse installation places the new structures in direct conflict with the old, almost as if they are shards of modernity spearing the ancient architectural orders. Admittedly, the Western world – in particular the vertical city – is understandably wary of proposals that seem to oppose the established order. Ando's proposal was far from antagonistic, however: it was a purely emotional architectural response to a remarkable city, the ultimate fantasy penthouse created as a celebration of height and visual drama.

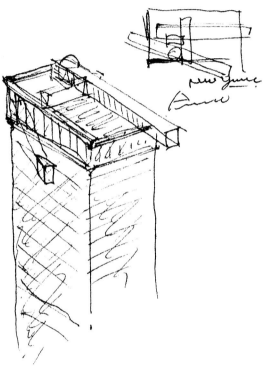

Above: **Penthouse in Manhattan.** Initial design sketch, showing how the organisational elements – two long diagonal interventions – were conceived right from the start

Right: **Penthouse in Manhattan.** The contemporary Manhattan skyline – the context for the project. New York's skyscrapers remain a hugely romantic image, especially for foreign visitors

Above: **Penthouse in Manhattan.** Model of the proposed scheme, illustrating the two vast glass pavilions and formal gardens at the peak of the structure

Left: **Penthouse in Manhattan.** Context model.
Treating the roof of the London Guarantee &
Accident Company Building as an element in a
modern landscape means that Ando's pavilions
float like the most isolated of country houses

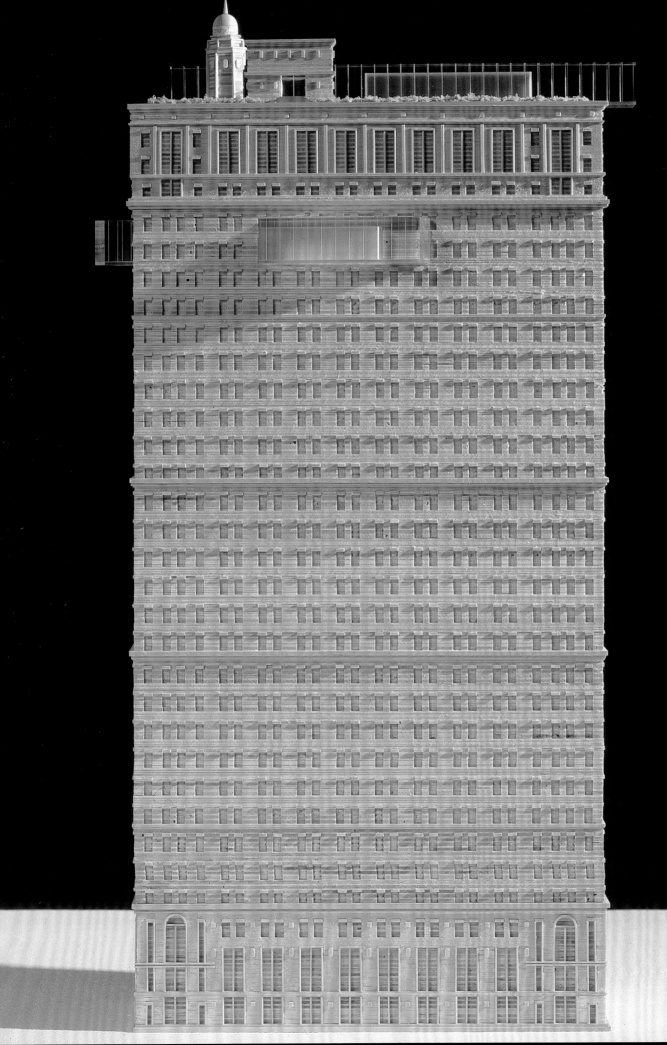

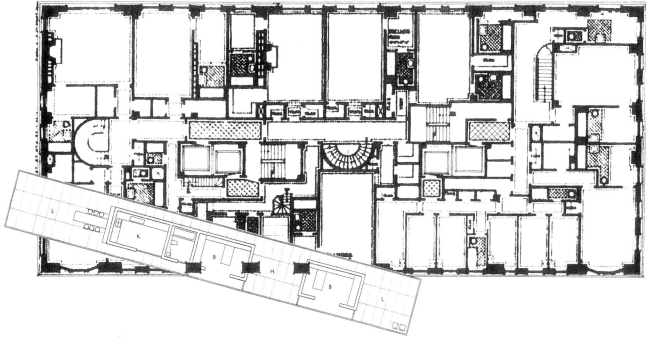

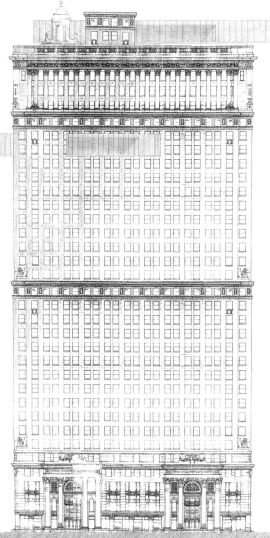

Above: **Penthouse in Manhattan.** Proposed floor plan: the new 'wedge' bears no relation to the existing plan, as if the building is to remain unoccupied and abandoned, a mere vessel for the new structure

Left: **Penthouse in Manhattan.** Elevation drawing. The architect is fascinated by the order and rhythms of the original facade, and uses the new structure to offset the precision

Opposite: **Penthouse in Manhattan.** The elevational view of the model dematerialises the impact of the glass pavilion on top and the 'wedge' of glass that seems to slice through the structure just below the upper floor. Nonetheless, this is a remarkably bold intervention

Left: **Penthouse in Manhattan.** Computer-generated view of the new rooftop pavilion. This is clearly intended as a meditative space, the reflecting pool dramatically doubling the dizzying array of lights on the horizon

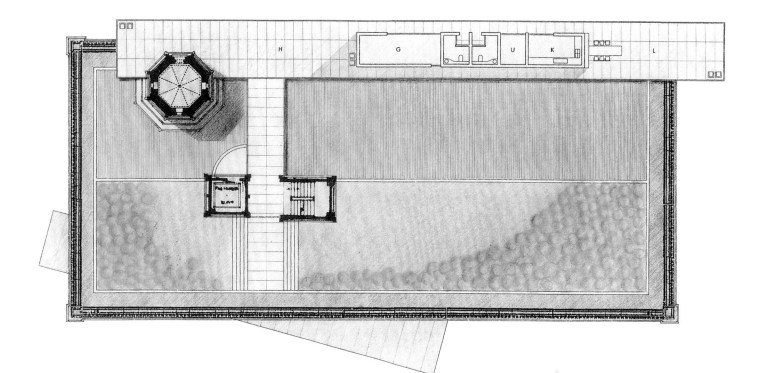

Above: **Penthouse in Manhattan.** The upper floor plan of the new structure is simplicity itself, a linear apartment with one bedroom, two huge living areas and views unlike any other in New York

Right: **Penthouse in Manhattan.** Side elevation. Like the top floor pavilion, the inserted 'wedge' cantilevers out into thin air

Opposite: **Penthouse in Manhattan.** The model

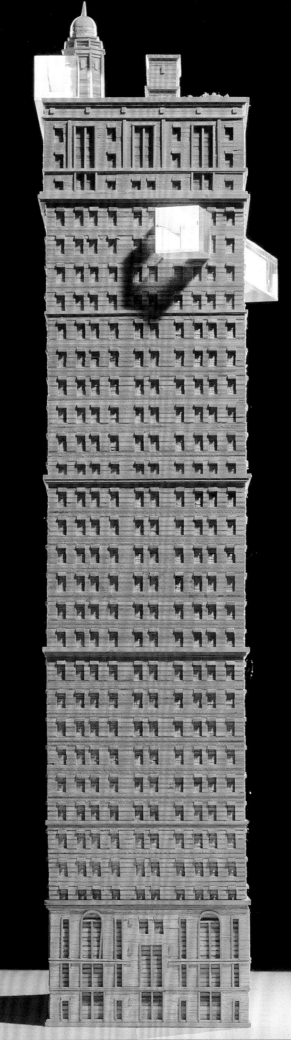

Kaufman Apartment

Simon Conder Associates

London 2000

Simon Conder's reworking of the upper floors of a 19th-century building in London's Shoreditch uses the penthouse pavilion as the focus for a reordered residential space. This apartment is an urban *pied-à-terre*, free from the restrictions placed on a full-time home. Essentially a one-bedroom apartment, the open-plan living arrangement on the lower level is enhanced by the addition of a new rooftop pavilion. This new upper storey not only contains the sleeping area for the apartment but also acts as a lantern, with the extensive use of glass and artificial lighting flooding the lower level with light.

The apartment is entered from an access walkway, past a study area and down into a kitchen/living room, where Conder's trademark purpose-designed furniture helps define the large areas of open space. Cupboard space is concealed within a long storage wall that runs the length of the apartment and, as on the kitchen cabinets, plain floor-to-ceiling doors are used throughout, without any visible handles or hinges. Artificial lighting is concealed beneath the new furniture, making the three sofa structures appear to float above the wooden floor.

A small terrace, screened by troughs planted with bamboo, opens off the sitting area. The principal architectural interventions on the lower floor are two obscure glass drums, one containing the WC and the other the shower. Lit by twin circular rooflights, the drums have curved glass doors that can be opened and joined to form a more conventional bathroom space.

The rooftop pavilion is reached via a cantilevered, oak staircase with a steel balustrade, leading up to a glass-floored bridge. Cross this and one reaches the bed area, with its custom-built wooden bed, floor-to-ceiling glazing and glass balustrades, all of which bring light down to the floor below, making the penthouse structure act as a lantern illuminating the rest of the apartment. Again, artificial light takes over after dark, illuminating the glass structures like the bridge and the bathroom drums.

The apartment is unusual in that the penthouse element is a space dedicated to sleeping rather than living. In this way, the feeling of space and openness generated by a high-level glass space is experienced at night-time, when the city roofs take on a very different quality. The new pavilion is shielded with bamboo screens and obscured glass from prying eyes in nearby structures and apartments, with only the two long views from each end of the pavilion preserved using clear glass. The architects describe the experience as 'having its own magic ... a private, detached capsule from which to experience the surrounding city lit up'.

Below: **Kaufman Apartment.** The main living space, with its custom-designed, built-in furniture. The kitchen can be seen behind, with the stair leading up to the sleeping area on the upper floor

Above: Kaufman Apartment. The bathroom is contained within two translucent glass drums, which can be opened up into the main living space or closed off as needs dictate. Toplit with natural daylight, they bring additional light into the lower floor

Left: Kaufman Apartment. The upper storey, or gallery level, viewed from the roof terrace with its iroko decking. A simple monopitch roof shields the master sleeping space

Opposite: Kaufman Apartment. The upper storey acts as a lantern, bringing light down into the living rooms below. The dining table is matched with a set of Hans Wegner's 'wishbone' chairs, the only furniture items in the apartment not designed by Simon Conder Associates

Primrose Hill Penthouse

David Connor Design

London 2003

This penthouse, designed by David Connor Design for the developers Span Group, sits atop a new development in London's Primrose Hill. Completed in 2003, the complex comprises offices, shops, a restaurant, four apartments and a penthouse – this last the showpiece of the development. The architects for the main structure, the London-based firm of Paskin Kyriakides Sands, worked within the constraints of an unusually shaped site, nearby rail lines and a mix of existing industrial buildings. The resulting £5 million building uses a variety of finishes, including an ordered street facade of geometrically precise brick, generous galvanised steel balconies and a glass, brick and wood panelled stair tower. Inside, the 464.5 square metre (5,000 square foot) space was fitted out by David Connor Design, Connor himself being no stranger to penthouse architecture. Together with Julian Powell-Tuck, he had created a dramatic penthouse overlooking Hyde Park, set high in the eaves of an existing Edwardian building, with an almost Gormenghast-like view of London's roofscape. Connor illustrated the structure with a spidery, almost Gothic drawing, exaggerating the perspective and uncanniness of this new landscape.

Despite occupying the second and third floors, this is the classic Modernist penthouse, a dramatic architectural statement crowning a building, grabbing all the best views for itself. The west and south walls are floor-to-ceiling glass, with a slender wooden-decked terrace running the length of the west side of the building, given privacy by careful planting. The curve of the zinc roof is mirrored by the smooth internal plaster finish, and the white-painted ceiling folds back in one continuous plane.

The kitchen, at the south of the upper floor, is illuminated by a large roof-light, while the stairwell, which features double-height windows, opens on to an east-facing, lower-storey terrace that is also accessible from the master-bedroom suite. The quality of the fixtures and fittings is extremely high for a speculative development; included are an integrated audiovisual system, air conditioning, electronically controlled blinds and curtains and a custom-designed lighting system. Bathrooms are finished with stone floors; wood floors are used elsewhere.

Connor's aesthetic is a refined form of Modernism – white walls, reductivist detailing and extensive use of glazing, both outside and inside, with the free-standing glass balustrading prompting the entire upper floor to be read as one continuous space. The external deck is at the same level as the interior floor, the glass assisting the sense of a seamless transition from inside to outside, a classic penthouse characteristic.

Above: **Primrose Hill Penthouse.** The external deck of the penthouse showing the unusual geometry of this upper floor apartment

Left: **Primrose Hill Penthouse.** The interior of David Connor Design's penthouse is arranged as a long living space. The kitchen, seen here, is illuminated from above by a skylight, while a terrace runs the full length of the building

Below: **Primrose Hill Penthouse.** Stairs lead to the bedrooms, an inversion of the traditional arrangement, used to maximise the light. The subtly curved white-painted roof scoops up light from the glazed wall and rooflights

Above: Primrose Hill Penthouse. The external deck at night. Natural shielding is provided by the lavender and ivy-filled planters

Right: Primrose Hill Penthouse. Located downstairs from the living area, the master bedroom is generously sized

Left and above: **Primrose Hill Penthouse.** Two views of the steel and wood staircase at the heart of the penthouse. The double-height space brings light down into the lower level and provides a focal point

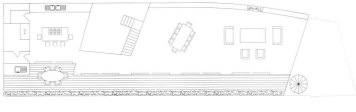

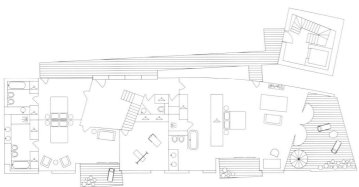

Above: **Primrose Hill Penthouse.** The upper and lower floors of the apartment

Kelly Penthouse

Lorcan O'Herlihy Architects

Marina del Rey, California 1997

Located in California's Marina del Rey, this two-storey, 180 square metre (1,930 square foot) penthouse is set on top of an existing apartment complex. The Kelly Penthouse is arranged as two distinct pavilions, a main residential component and a separate games room/office pavilion, a small steel-framed structure with a glass skin of vertical, Reglit-style glass channels forming the walls. The external walkway from the master bedroom is shielded from the Californian sun by a wooden, slatted trellis.

The main residential area is characterised by an open plan and an emphasis on the views to the Pacific Ocean. Services, like the kitchen, bathrooms and toilets, are situated along the south wall of the long, thin floor plan, enabling the architects to open up the living/dining area on the lower floor and the master bedroom on the upper floor to the views. As well as the decked walk to the games room/office, there is a catwalk, reflecting the loft's slender floor plan, leading from the master bedroom through the double-height void above the living area to a private deck from which the owner can look out over the beach and watch the sunset.

The detached games room/office pavilion is a crucial part of the penthouse mythology, a free-standing element that recalls both the historic origins of the penthouse structure and the Modernist house as a pristine object within the landscape, despite the penthouse's relatively low-rise status.

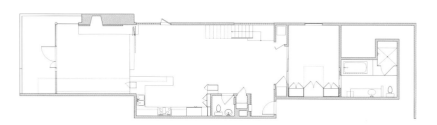

Left from top: **Kelly Penthouse.** Second and first floor plans

Below: **Kelly Penthouse.** The deck in the
Californian sun. The walkway provides a shady
route to the games room/office

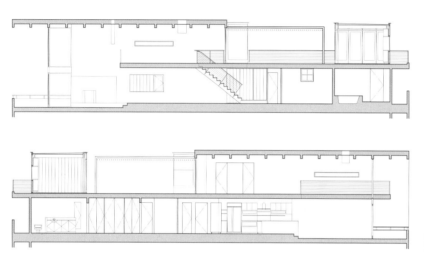

Above: **Kelly Penthouse.** Longitudinal sections

Right: **Kelly Penthouse.** The games room, a free-standing, glass-walled pavilion atop the Kelly residence. Like a personal retreat, the room is also an office and a sanctuary – a penthouse atop a penthouse

Above: **Kelly Apartment.** Shower area situated along the south wall of the apartment

Left: **Kelly Apartment.** Classic Californian Modernism meets the penthouse. The double-height living area is flanked by a catwalk above, leading to a tiny, secluded roof terrace with an ocean view

Bermondsey Penthouse

Blauel Architects

London 2000

Blauel Architects' small penthouse takes a three-storey building and transforms it with the addition of a penthouse pavilion. Located in Bermondsey, south London, the original building was a warehouse converted into a live/work space during the first major push to create a residential living area in this part of the city.

The client was also the contractor, and this arrangement defined the use of metal as the primary building material, a material with which the client, Robin Greenwood, was very familiar from his work as a sculptor. This familiarity meant that Blauel's design could use exposed structural elements safe in the knowledge that they would be treated as fundamental to its aesthetic look. The result is a classic 'rooftop pavilion', a metal-clad structure with steel louvres and a curved aluminium roof of German design. The architects admit that 'such an aesthetic might be more expected in a drier, warmer climate', but the extensive use of insulation and the ability of the louvres on the south facade of the penthouse to shield against solar gain, as well as provide privacy, combine to create a light, airy structure.

The new structure is surrounded by a wooden terrace. An open-plan kitchen and living space on the upper storey sit beneath the shallow metal roof vault, their fixtures and furnishings chosen for their industrial, metallic feel, like the catering cooker and the dining table. Installation of floor-to-ceiling, sliding glass windows with views across to the City of London was made viable by the stiffness of the structure. Down from the steel-framed stairs with their wooden treads, the lower level is more formal, mixing work space with sleeping areas.

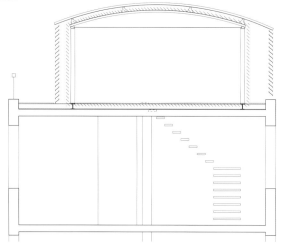

Left: Bermondsey Penthouse. Section through the Bermondsey Penthouse, showing the addition of the barrel-vaulted roof

Left: **Bermondsey Penthouse.** A detail of the carefully finished metalwork that characterises this penthouse apartment; the client, a sculptural metalworker, was also the primary contractor

Below: **Bermondsey Penthouse.** Viewed from afar, the penthouse presents itself as a neat, distinguished finishing element to the existing warehouse building. The metal louvres create a distinctive silhouette

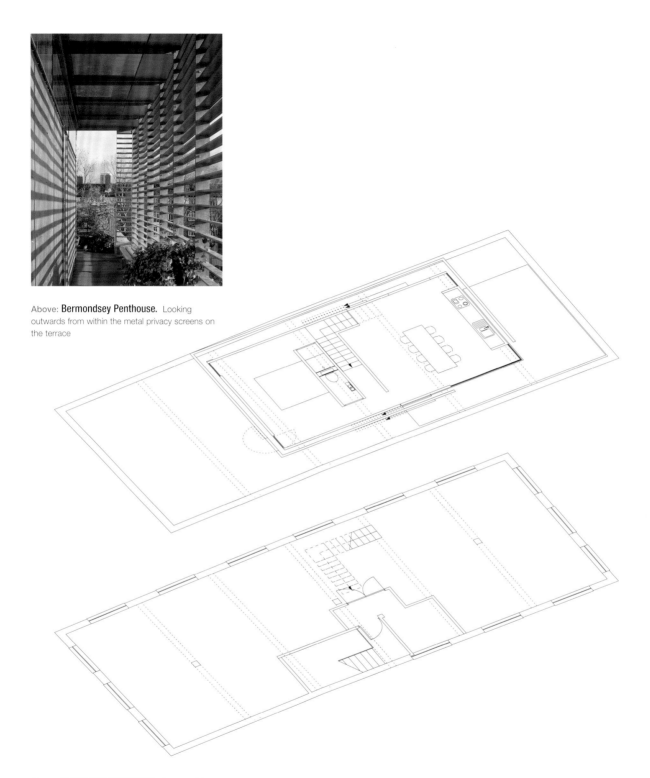

Above: **Bermondsey Penthouse.** Looking outwards from within the metal privacy screens on the terrace

Above: **Bermondsey Penthouse.** Axonometric views of the two-storey penthouse, illustrating the way the smaller pavilion, with its single bedroom and kitchen/dining area, sits above a far larger open-plan floor below, given over to offices and work spaces

Opposite: **Bermondsey Penthouse.** Inside the penthouse, the living arrangements are reversed: open-plan living space on the upper floor and offices below. The scale is modest, and the detailing simple – no need for expensive, sleek kitchen units or built-in furniture

Greenwich Street Project

Archi-Tectonics

New York 2003

Archi-Tectonics's 7,153 square metre (77,000 square foot) Greenwich Street Project, on the edge of SoHo, is a bold addition to the New York skyline. This total reconstruction of an old six-storey warehouse creates 22 residential lofts arranged above gallery and retail spaces, so adding five storeys to the site.

Led by Winka Dubbeldam, Archi-Tectonics have used a remarkable approach to address the city's zoning codes. The entire front of the building is a glass curtain wall, subtly unfolding and enveloping the existing, refurbished structure. The architects describe it as a 'suspended waterfall' of glass which cascades around the original six-storey building, the zone between the two marked off by a series of cantilevered balconies. The 'folding' glass facade reinterprets the city's strict setback codes, integrating the legal requirements within a flowing facade (which flares out at ground floor level to become a canopy), in contrast to the emphasis on stepped horizontal elements of the more traditional roofscape. Lifts and utilities have been tidied into a central core, knitting the old and new sections of the building together.

Naturally, the new loft apartments have been left as blank canvases; grey concrete walls and floors, hardwood windows and acres of space allow design-savvy New Yorkers to create their own space (while still retaining a full quota of electronic information systems). On the upper levels, the traditional setback allows for the creation of a full-width terrace, providing views across to the Hudson River. The penthouse terrace on the 11th floor has unobstructed 360-degree views of lower Manhattan.

The building, which was engineered by Buro Happold, with Israel Berger & Associates the key consultants on the curtain wall, represents a contemporary interpretation of the classic ziggurat apartment form. Instead of stone-clad solidity, it plays with the transparent qualities of the International Style. New York is hardly lacking in prime examples of these genres, but the Greenwich Street Project provides a modern interpretation of the traditional penthouse-crowned structure, albeit far removed from the Fifth Avenue stomping ground of the original prototypes. At night, the structure gives off an Art Deco glow, evoking the floodlit verticality of the interwar period.

The Greenwich Street Project inverts the contemporary approach to penthouse building. Whereas the Modernist penthouse is, for the most part, an unwieldy accretion or an architectural afterthought driven by economic logic, Archi-Tectonics have melded the traditional penthouse's *raison d'être* – the setback laws – with the best of Modernist design. It seems fitting that this structure should be constructed in New York, home of the original penthouse.

Above: **Greenwich Street Project.** A computer-generated view of the external facade of the new building, which follows the classic New York stepped setback profile

Above: **Greenwich Street Project.** The proposed new lobby, an apartment building entrance in the grand style

Right: **Greenwich Street Project.** A rendering illustrating the view to the Hudson River and Lower Manhattan from the upper storey terrace. The terrace is placed between two layers of the glass curtain wall

Above: **Greenwich Street Project.** Computer-generated section illustrating the way the glass curtain wall folds across the structure, altering the dynamic feel of each individual apartment

Left: **Greenwich Street Project.** A computer-generated drawing showing the glass curtain wall folding across the entire structure

Left: **Greenwich Street Project.** Computer-generated section of the building

Left: **Greenwich Street Project.** The aerial view showing the rear of the building

Above: **Greenwich Street Project.** Rendering illustrating the glass curtain wall

SIXTH FLOOR PLAN:
5 loft space
6 kitchenette
7 bath
8 elevator-stair core
9 balcony

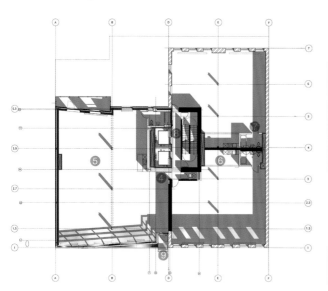

Above: Greenwich Street Project. Floor plan and artist's impression of a typical open loft in the new building, illustrating how the accommodation is arranged around the new central elevator core

MAIN FLOOR PLAN:
1 art gallery
2 office space
3 retail
4 entry

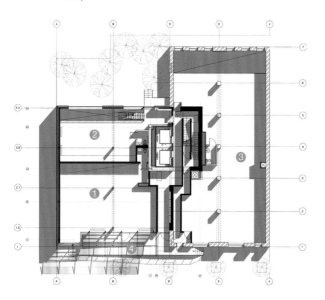

Above: Greenwich Street Project. Floor plan and artist's impression of a proposed art gallery space on the ground floor of the building

Above: **Greenwich Street Project.** An exploded
perspective view of the way the old and new are
intertwined

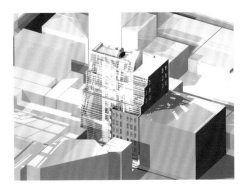

Above: **Greenwich Street Project.** Axonometric view of
the project and its relationship to the surrounding
streetscape. The five new storeys are especially clear

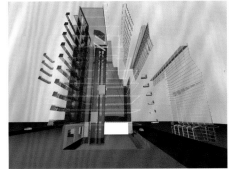

Above: **Greenwich Street Project.** This exploded view
illustrates the addition of the new glass curtain wall and
cedar-clad galleries to the existing structure, transforming it
into a very contemporary building

Grassi Penthouse

OBR Architetti Associati

Grassi, Italy 2005

The Grassi Penthouse has been designed by OBR (Open Building Research), a studio founded in 2000 by Paolo Brescia and Tommaso Principi, both former members of the Renzo Piano Building Workshop. The 10-strong studio, based in Genoa, is working on a number of residential and commercial projects, and the scheme for the Grassi Penthouse is relatively small.

The architects describe the penthouse, placed atop a 1950s apartment building, as a design based on the 'constant relationship between inside space and outside space'. The accommodation is arranged as a series of enclosed and introspective spaces that gradually become more open as they lead towards the exterior. There are five key modular elements – living, eating, sleeping, washing and storage – and these extend outwards from the service core which contains the stair and bathroom areas. Living and sleeping areas lead from this core, each with its own terrace flowing outwards through the space to the rooftops beyond.

The traditional city has never been as hospitable to the penthouse form as the modern metropolis. At Grassi, the outlook is a roofscape of tile and slate, with external planting helping to obscure the sense of an inside/outside world. The greenery creates scenic views from the interior even when the roofs are obscured, and gives the impression of an isolated dwelling shielded from its urban location. The same materials are used inside as out – a limited palette including ardesia stone, free-flowing timber decking and steel.

Left: Grassi Penthouse. Artist's impression. The open-plan space conceals its urban location with a forest of greenery on the twin terraces

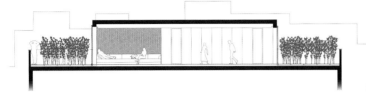

Left: **Grassi Penthouse.** Section through the penthouse

Above: **Grassi Penthouse.** Computer-generated image of the interior – a space that blends seamlessly into a traditional skyline

Left: **Grassi Penthouse.** Floor plan

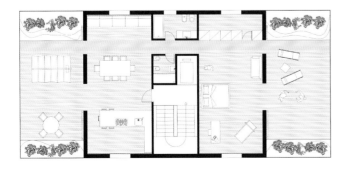

Stingel Apartment

Cha & Innerhofer

New York 2001

The Stingel Apartment and Rooftop Pavilion adapts and upgrades the traditional New York apartment building to the rank of penthouse, bringing elements of Upper West Side style to the more down-to-earth East Village. Located on the floor of a five-storey brick town house, it offers views of the nearby Saint Mark's Church.

Paul Cha and Margaret Innerhofer's firm first undertook renovation work for their artist client in 1998, returning three years later to create a wooden pavilion and deck that integrate with the modest 65 square metre (700 square foot) living space below. The roof is graced by a 32.5 square metre (350 square foot) pavilion, providing the artist with a view encompassing the icons of the Manhattan cityscape, from the Chrysler Building in the north to Battery Park City in the south.

The architects describe the pavilion 'as a refuge above the surrounding cityscape', an object in a manmade landscape. Wood is used extensively, and the whole feel of the project is one of a calm oasis in the midst of an often chaotic and unstable cityscape.

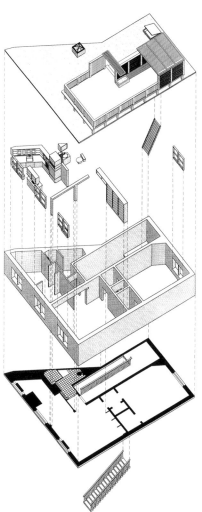

Above: **Stingel Apartment.** Exploded axonometric

Left: **Stingel Apartment.** After first refurbishing the upper storey of this Manhattan apartment, the architects returned three years later to create a bespoke deck area above

Left: **Stingel Apartment.** The design makes extensive use of wood, for seating, privacy screens and sun-shaders

Below: **Stingel Apartment.** Manhattan unfurls before your eyes, even from the enclosed seating area

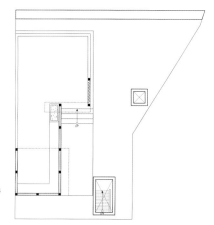
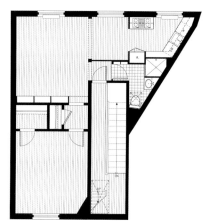

Right: **Stingel Apartment.** Roof and apartment plans

Below: **Stingel Apartment.** View of the deck area

Above: **Stingel Apartment.** A general view of the
interior of this typical New York residence, renovated
by Cha & Innerhofer in 1998

West Village Penthouse

Christoff:Finio Architecture

New York 2003

Penthouses need not be sprawling duplexes or triplexes. The origin of the name – for a modest shack-like structure that originally housed the protruding elevator room – belies the undeniable aura of glamour afforded to the great interwar apartments, an enduring legacy that has led to the current era's demand for cutting-edge spectacle.

Just occasionally, however, a penthouse apartment is constructed on a smaller scale, emphasising its location, separation and distinctness from the 'host structure'. At just 464.5 square metres (500 square feet), this West Village penthouse is in fact a residential extension, a vertical expansion to the roofline to reclaim a favourite view before it was eclipsed by New York's still-rampaging skyline. Ironically, the two new towers that block the existing view are Richard Meier's Perry Street Towers, two residential apartment towers in the architect's trademark glass and steel idiom which mark a return to the classic glamour of the apartment building. Perry Street features prominent double-height penthouses, one of which, a triplex, was reportedly bought by the fashion mogul Calvin Klein for $14 million.

The West Village penthouse is an altogether more modest affair, an addition that aims to better its upscale usurper. New York-based practice Christoff:Finio Architecture, founded in 1998 by Martin Finio and Taryn Christoff, specialises in residential development that ekes out new views, spaces and interpretations of the city. Initial concept renders and sketches illustrate the West Village penthouse being 'dropped' on to the existing building, recalling the iconic image of the model of Le Corbusier's Unité d'Habitation, one living unit 'pulled' from the facade to show the way the building was composed of a system of interlocking components. Christoff:Finio have created a classic Modernist steel-framed box perched on the top of an existing three-storey 19th-century structure.

Horizontal and vertical blinds automatically extend to cover the outdoor section of decking at the front of the new penthouse. Even though the new structure is a prominent addition, 'clipped' to the original building, its form is still dictated by the building codes, which determine how much of the facade can be glazed. The new penthouse is reached by a broad stairwell, which also acts as a means of bringing natural light into the rear of the apartment below. A window on the west wall of the structure creates a new view back towards Manhattan, opening up a vista previously unavailable to the apartment. The added height means that the Hudson River will continue to glisten on the client's horizon – the perfect allusion to classic penthouse style.

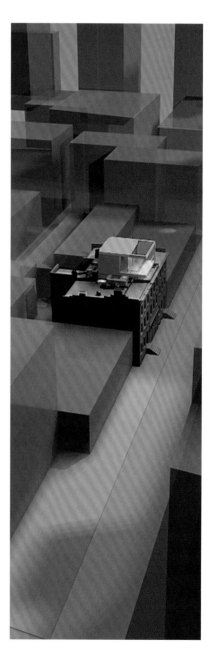

Above: West Village Penthouse. Context rendering, illustrating the modest scale of the new penthouse

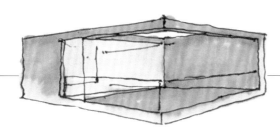

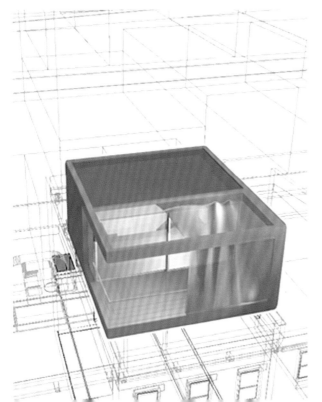

Top: **West Village Penthouse.** Early concept sketch of the West Village Penthouse

Above: **West Village Penthouse.** The new penthouse, shown adjacent to Richard Meier's Perry Street Towers development

Left: **West Village Penthouse.** The main component of the West Village Penthouse is this residential cube, shielded from prying eyes by a vertical and horizontal curtain that can close off the external deck

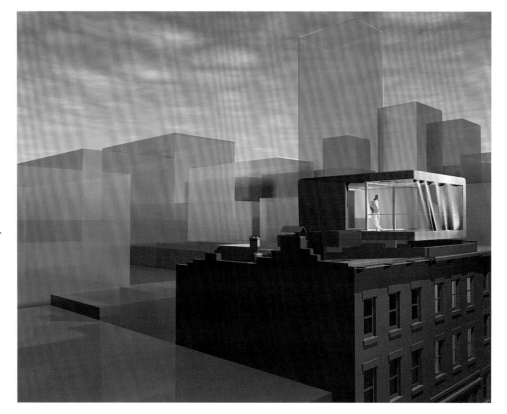

Right: West Village Penthouse.
Distinct and prominent above
the original building below, the
West Village Penthouse is an
uncompromising attempt to
maximise space in one of the
most densely populated cities
on the planet

**Below: West Village
Penthouse.** With the horizontal
motorised curtains drawn, the
penthouse offers a little patch of
New York sky for private
contemplation

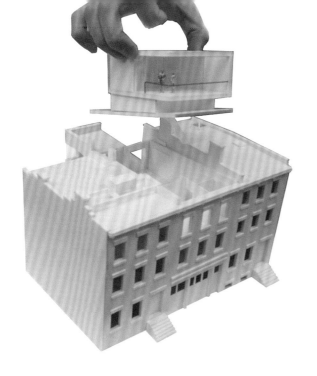

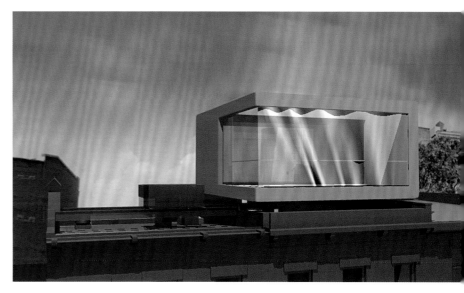

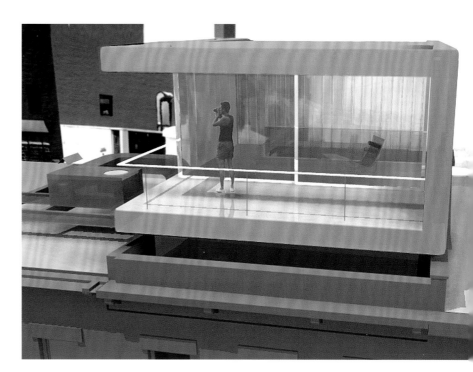

Above right: **West Village Penthouse.** Two views of the apartment, curtains closed and open. The terrace is generous, given the size of the penthouse, which is raised up off the existing roof to maximise views

Above left: **West Village Penthouse.** These model shots illustrates the new addition being 'slotted' into place

Two Rooftop Houses

Pierre d'Avoine Architects

London 2000–3

The penthouse offers a privileged view of an otherwise unseen landscape, the roofscape. Yet relatively few modern penthouses specifically address the site conditions of the structure they inhabit. Located in Fulham, west London, the Piper Building was constructed in 1961 as an office and laboratory building for the Gas Board. Its most distinguished feature was a large mural by the artist John Piper, which was retained and restored when the structure was converted to private flats by the architects Lifschutz Davidson. The entire building was overhauled, with a reclad exterior and the addition of new metal balconies hung from the roof.

The building's new use, complete with updated individual services, resulted in the two plant buildings on the flat roof becoming redundant. Working in conjunction with the developer, architect Pierre d'Avoine was invited to bring these original 'penthouses' back to life – and commercial viability. D'Avoine was intrigued by the landscape of the roof, drawing comparisons between the stony beach at the south coast settlement of Dungeness and the pebble-strewn, object-littered space. Each apartment below was allocated a small section of roof, and the random collection of possessions and furniture that has accumulated there has given it a similar character to the makeshift beachside huts and structures one finds at the seaside. Perversely, the empty rooftop also fitted the definition of a 'brownfield site', inner-city locations specifically targeted by a government initiative for the building of more homes.

D'Avoine's response was to convert the plant rooms into two 'houses', Rooftop East and Rooftop West, using a combination of prefabricated techniques and traditional in situ construction. The bare bones of the existing structures were reused, and eight steel-framed modules, devised by the engineers Atelier One and built offsite in a factory, were manoeuvred into position by crane. The steelwork was then clad and rendered to present the outward appearance of a monolithic block on one side, with extensive glazing to make the most of dramatic views across the River Thames on the other. Additional privacy is also provided by an external skin formed by filmy screens of stainless-steel gauze. This industrial product is designed to obscure and conceal the rooftop structures, rendering their forms vague and indistinct against the sky.

The resulting penthouses exist in a world of their own, their vague form crystallising, as one approaches, to almost merge with the very functional, rigid grid of the roof with its jumble of servicing and structural elements. Inside,

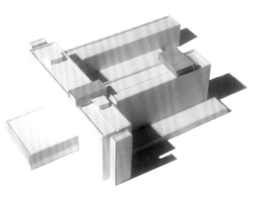

Above: **Two Rooftop Houses**. Before-and-after models illustrating the extent of the new works on the existing Piper Building

Right: **Two Rooftop Houses**. The 1961 Piper Building seen from a distance, showing the two new 'houses', adrift in their own private landscape

Below: **Two Rooftop Houses**. Rooftop West (left), and Rooftop East. The Piper Building's roofscape is chaotic and disjointed, an environment unlike that of a conventional residential project

floor-to-ceiling windows and raised-up floor levels make Rooftops East and West appear to float, distinct and aloof from their surroundings. The two Rooftops were speculative developments, so internal finishings were kept deliberately simple: wooden floors, white walls and an absence of skirtings and mouldings. Both houses are characterised by an open-plan upper floor living space incorporating a kitchen/dining area, living room and master bedroom, with a more conventional arrangement of smaller rooms below.

Right: **Two Rooftop Houses**. The steel frames for the new houses were constructed offsite and craned on to the rooftops, where they were fitted out

Below: **Two Rooftop Houses**. A photomontage of the design at an early stage, conveying the shimmering presence the architect was trying to achieve

Above: **Two Rooftop Houses**. Rooftop West, with the River Thames beyond

Right: **Two Rooftop Houses**. Rooftop East and West were fabricated in Manchester before being transported south to the site

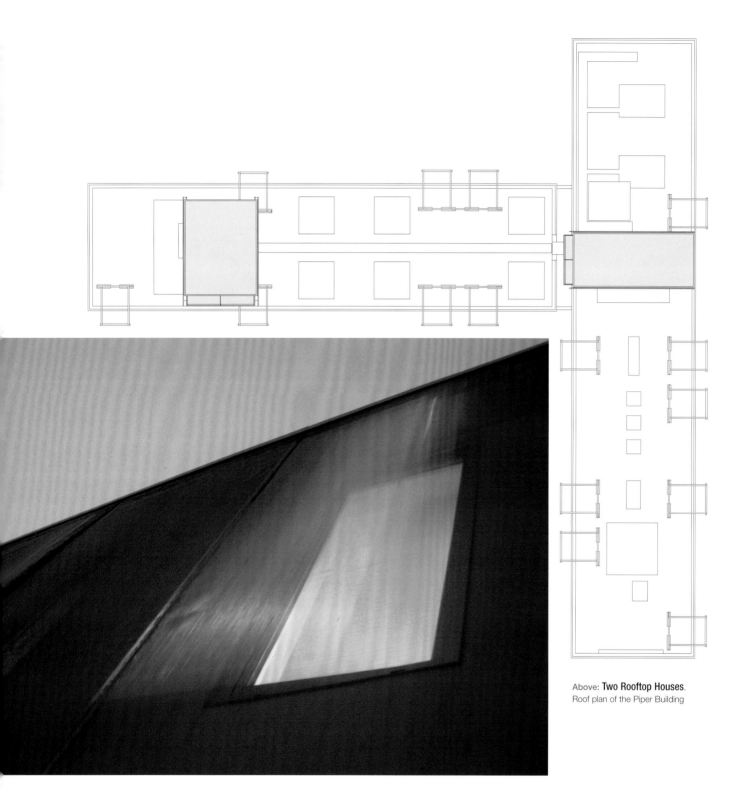

Above: **Two Rooftop Houses**.
Roof plan of the Piper Building

Above: **Two Rooftop Houses**. Rooftop East, the
gauzy metal screen illuminated from within

Above: **Two Rooftop Houses**. Two views of Rooftop East at night

Left: **Two Rooftop Houses**. The bathroom on the upper floor of Rooftop East. Fixtures and fittings were kept low-key

Left: **Two Rooftop Houses**. Rooftop West appears perched above the existing building

Camden Penthouse

A-EM Studio

London 2000

This penthouse flat in north London takes the classic pavilion-on-the-rooftop approach, bringing a fresh view of a hitherto concealed urban situation. Located in Camden, where gentrification and deprivation have been jostling for many decades, A-EM Studio's rooftop pavilion is modest and unassuming, deriving its spatial qualities from the open-plan living area, large expanses of glass and fixtures and fittings that allow for through views in three directions.

Designed by Glyn Emrys and Pascal Madoc-Jones of A-EM Studios, the new structure sits on top of an 'undistinguished' 1970s apartment building. Given the low-rise quality of much of the city, the architects believe that 'London's rooftops represent a hardly explored level of inhabitation above the traffic and grime of the streets'. The new penthouse offers 'a new perspective on the urban environment impossible to imagine from the confines of ground level living and tightly bounded back gardens'.

Camden Road is busy and generally uninspiring, the usual accretion of various styles and functions. The view from the roof consists of a collection of objects: church spires, the spotlights for a nearby football stadium, gasometers and neighbouring blocks. Looking further beyond, one can see the green hills of north London's lungs: Hampstead and Highgate.

To create the new penthouse, A-EM first had to reconfigure the former upper floor of the building, adding another flight of stairs to the existing common parts to create a new entrance. The penthouse is divided into two distinct zones, a more enclosed sleeping area containing two bedrooms and a bathroom close to the entrance to the apartment, and a more open-plan living area at the front. A large area of wooden deck terracing extends all around the penthouse.

The flat is designed as a lightweight and economical construction: key elements, such as the ceiling-hung fireplace and furniture that sits off the ground, preserve the views and airy character of the space.

Above and opposite: **Camden Penthouse.** Six views of the interior and the terrace. Its open-plan living area, extensive glazing and lightweight furniture enhance and expand views outwards and across the space

Above: **Camden Penthouse.** External view

Left: **Camden Penthouse.** Floor plan illustrating the open-plan livng area and the more enclosed, private bedrooms behind

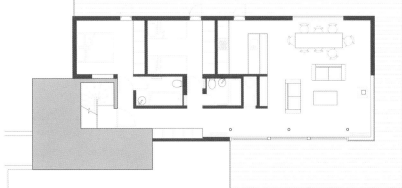

First Penthouse London Projects

First Penthouse Limited

Albert Court
St John's Wood Court

Annika and Hakan Olsson's First Penthouse company, established in 1992, retro-engineers London's residential building stock, blending advanced construction methods with a hard-nosed look at how to exploit the most desirable real estate. First Penthouse has designed a relatively cheap, prefabricated module, which the two engineers (also husband and wife) use to create instant structures on the capital's empty roofs. These are penthouses that are designed to blend seamlessly into the traditional architecture of the 'host' building.

For the most part, the results aren't visually innovative architecture – this is the whole point. Ironically, though, the extensive use of prefabrication and the emphasis on speed and quality mean that it is far more high-tech than the traditional methods used to build many modern buildings. Mobile cranes can achieve an ever cheaper transition from factory to rooftop and costly high-level construction is avoided.

Each First Penthouse design is perfectly tailored for its environment, disguised as a mansard or even a Modernist box. The bespoke prefabricated units are cunningly designed to blend with their host locations, be they existing Edwardian apartment buildings or contemporary loft developments. By picking modest yet high-yield sites in some of London's most prestigious residential areas, the costs of fabrication and installation are easily offset by the significant market value of a finished penthouse. Kitchens, bathrooms and interior decorations are installed in advance, enabling the entire structure to be fixed in place in a single day.

Having negotiated the air rights to the roof space, First Penthouse custom-designs each unit to suit the building. For the aforementioned Edwardian block, the design mimicked the high mansarded roofs typical of the era. More contemporary designs, such as the pavilion that sits on a roof terrace at the Bankside Loft development on London's South Bank, can also be accommodated.

The Swedish factory that manufactures the units is about as far removed from penthouse glamour as possible – it usually fabricates McDonald's restaurants, perhaps the most fast-track constructions on the planet. Subtle touches are added to blend the new with the old, such as reusing existing roof tiles, while such elements as services are aligned to ensure a seamless connection. Although the speed of construction undoubtedly helps with gaining permissions, First Penthouse still has to contend with the notoriously arcane British planning system and a host of regulations, not to

Right: **Albert Court.** This new set of penthouses created atop London's Albert Court is designed to blend seamlessly with the existing period building

Opposite top: **Albert Court.** A prefabricated mansard module is craned into place atop Albert Court

Opposite bottom: **St John's Wood Court.** An Edwardian mansion block, is extended by a new First Penthouse mansard roof

mention tracing, requesting and purchasing air rights leases.

The series of five penthouses on Albert Court in Kensington, a handsome Queen Anne Revival red-brick Edwardian mansion block adjacent to the Royal Albert Hall, has been designed to resemble an existing mansard. The new units are steeply raked at the front of the building and carefully incorporate the existing towering chimneys to give the impression that the penthouses, which range in size from 270 to 372 square metres (2,900 to 4,000 square feet), have always been a part of the building. Large dormer windows are set into the mansard, while the rear of each new unit opens on to the existing light well.

A scheme atop St John's Wood Court, a slightly later mansion block, is less complex in its design response to the existing building, featuring one high mansarded section and a smaller, pavilion-like structure tucked away out of sight behind the roofline. There are also more modern stand-alone designs, such as the unit designed for a large terrace at the Bankside Lofts.

First Penthouse has surveyed London's unused roofscapes as part of its business plan and located around 700 potential sites for its prefabricated units, acres of hugely expensive airborne real estate currently lying empty. While other schemes for prefabricated penthouses exist (notably the LoftCube and the m-house), only First Penthouse take a chameleon-like approach, camouflaging their creations among the rooftops. In a notoriously conservative housing market, when faced with the choice between a costly but bold architectural statement and an uncontroversial continuation of what already exists, it's little wonder that the First Penthouse method is so successful.

Above and right: **Albert Court.** An unashamedly commercial operation, First Penthouse identifies suitable 'plots' in areas of high property value, gains the necessary permissions and develops units for resale at the maximum possible price. The standard of interior fixtures and fittings is high, but conventional; this is not about innovating

Left: **St John's Wood Court.** Before and after at St John's Wood Court, demonstrating the way in which a framework is laid out on the existing flat roof to receive the 'penthouse' components

Opposite top: **Albert Court.** An enclosed roof garden has been created at this London project, surrounded by the mansard components that make up the new apartments

Opposite bottom: **St John's Wood Court.** A new penthouse addition at St John's Wood Court, north London

The Future

In all likelihood, the penthouse will continue to represent the apex of urban living. Depending on whether one has an optimistic or pessimistic view of the future, the penthouse will prevail over a utopian or dystopian tomorrow. In the dystopic vision, the penthouse with its eyrie-like status atop the city, looking down on the world below, will become a rich man's fortress. In a future world of greater and greater social inequality, the penthouse, housed in unattainable peaks, would be increasingly shielded from the gritty realities of everyday life – not just a retreat from participating at street level, but a retreat from society itself.

The second vision is democratic, envisioning a future high-rise architecture that rejects the penthouse's alpha status and proposes that its defining and most attractive characteristics – expansive views, generous terraces and capacious living area – are those most suitable for universal application. In short, we should *all* be living in penthouses, usurping the traditionally rigid planning of high-rise buildings in favour of a more sprawling, ziggurat-like urban landscape where the joys of penthouse living are available to everyone. This is a view that has been espoused, with varying degrees of

The Future

success, from the earliest days of Modernism, but it has taken nearly 80 years to remove aesthetics from the intellectual argument, leaving density the only element to tackle. Could the 'penthouse' be a model for mass-market, high-density living? Rather than limit the sense of openness generated by the penthouse's status as a unique, isolated object, careful planning of relatively low-rise developments ensures that everyone gets a view and a sense of visual drama with their apartment. Amsterdam-based Tangram Architekten's De Kamp project, due for completion in 2005, exemplifies the trend for complex high-density living, eschewing vertical stacking for a more free-form arrangement of living components.

The recognition that rooftop spaces make effective gardens – even farms – and that such green roofs are also environmentally beneficial might pave the way for vertical cities where all functions, not just living and working, are stacked, effectively democratising the nature of high-rise space. The Rotterdam-based firm MVRDV's project Pig City is a radical reimagining of how the Netherlands' pork exports might be stacked, automated and compacted, freeing up former agricultural land for residential and recreational use. MVRDV is just one of a group of European practices writing and theorising about urban density. Their manifesto-like FARMAX,[1] published in 1998, included a scheme for a 'Stacked Park' (later manifested as the Dutch

De Kamp, Amsterdam-Buitenveldert Apartments Tangram Architekten Amsterdam

Penthouses are not the most democratic of urban spaces, yet their lofty perch enables them to conjure up light-filled, airy interiors that belie their central location and the high density of the surrounding housing. Amsterdam-based firm Tangram Architekten has taken two of the penthouse's most enviable characteristics – the terrace and extensive glazing – and translated them into a building of 38 'stacked' penthouse apartments. The architects stress the project is about 'the power of space between built masses', breaking down four structures into sculptural forms that form a landscape of carefully structured views, including a glazed winter garden. External spaces, both public and private, are extensive, as if the ground had been lifted up and fragmented by an organic building.

Many Modernist architects used the balcony and terrace as pivotal devices, allowing the rigorous geometry of their buildings to spill out into the surrounding environment. In the work of the American Paul Rudolph or the Frenchman Jean Renaudie (especially the latter's housing project in Ivry), a generous balcony became integral to the design, rather than a tacked-on afterthought to decorate the facade. A traditional penthouse typically has more outside space than an apartment and the Tangram scheme, due for completion in 2005, exploits both the free-form nature of the penthouse apartment and the undeniable attractions of the word itself.

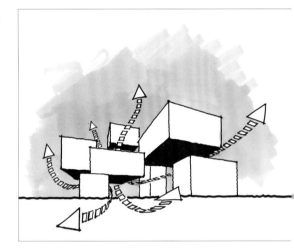

Pig City MVRDV

The Netherlands is the European Union's largest exporter of pig meat. But how can this pork production line be streamlined and modernised? MVRDV, a firm known for their emphasis on intensive research and presentation, created Pig City as a means of demonstrating the high rise's potential as a tool for solving problems of density, simultaneously calling into question the very same issues of quality of life that have dogged the residential tower since its inception. This porcine utopia proposed 76 towers of over 610 metres (2,000 feet), with a 90 metre x 90 metre (300 x 300 foot) floor plan, giving each inhabitant plenty of space to wallow. Pig City is, naturally, only a concept. But, more importantly, it is a concept steeped in critical thinking, a stern warning about what might lie ahead should Modernist principles be applied on purely economic grounds and not ethical ones. The parallels with humankind's ongoing flirtation with high-rise utopias are explicit

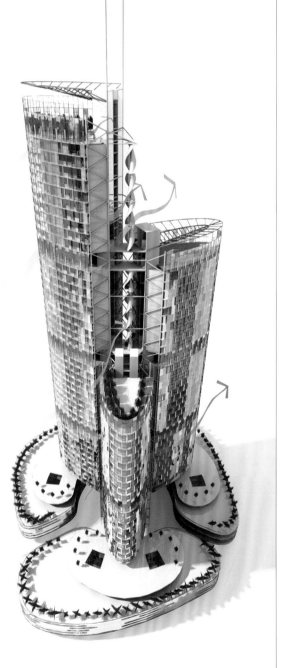

Skyhouse Concept Marks Barfield Architects London

The Skyhouse is a residential concept from Marks Barfield Architects, best known as the creators of the London Eye. There is continual pressure from central government for new housing initiatives, but little official encouragement for new high-density schemes, and Skyhouse was developed as a means of demonstrating that living in towers need not bring back unpleasant memories of the original tower blocks. Given recent emphasis on high-quality residential towers for high-end private buyers, the economies of scale led the architects to believe that high rise still offers a positive solution for social housing.

The Skyhouse is about sustainable high-rise living, affordable apartments that are not simply pitched at young professionals, but at key workers, young families and empty nesters. A modular design, which can be scaled in accordance with the demands and restrictions on the site, the Skyhouse comprises three habitable 'petals' accessed from a central core. Publicly accessible gardens are spaced evenly up the structure, and provision is made for commercial and community space. With the largest version of the concept housing 500 units, the intention is to find a suitable site and keep costs down, eschewing the contemporary view that a successful tower is usually the domain of the rich.

pavilion at the 2000 Hanover Expo), and the WoZoCo's apartment building in Amsterdam constructed in 1997. The latter maximised its site with a series of huge wood-clad cantilevers, each containing additional apartments.

At various stages in modern architecture's eclectic path between the Scylla of social responsibility and the Charybdis of the corporate client, both utopian and dystopian versions of the penthouse's future have been played out in concepts, schemes and even built designs. Democratic high-rise living for all was the theme of SITE Architects' tongue-in-cheek proposal for a suburban street restructured as a downtown high rise, with each plot-perfect bungalow and tract home arranged in a vertical grid. SITE's ironic solution for democratising the high rise highlighted the paradox of vertical living: that what was initially intended to promote social equality served only to distance the haves from the have-nots. The London-based studio FAT (Fashion Architecture Taste) demonstrated a similar take on the new vertical community with their competition entry for the regeneration of two existing tower blocks in Plaistow, east London. Other schemes take a more practical approach. The British firm of Marks Barfield envisages a socially democratic high-rise structure called the Skyhouse, with a series of gardens in the sky acting as social and recreational spaces in a tower of affordable housing units. The architect Bill Dunster's Flower Tower takes a similarly green approach, integrating wind turbines into the petal-shaped plan, with the upper floors given over to communal activities and not to the remote, more spacious apartments of a lucky few.

Above: **East London Tower Blocks.** FAT's competition entry for the recladding of existing tower blocks in Plaistow, east London. Deliberately referential, iconoclastic and irreverent, FAT (fashion, architecture, taste) reinvent the high rise as a compendium of familiar domestic forms and motifs

Regardless of such optimism, the utopian high rise faces seemingly insurmountable difficulties, not least a system that continues to place high-quality high-rise architecture at the very top of the social and financial tree. Opening up the sky will face stiff opposition. The corporate penthouse, that great innovation of early 20th-century Wall Street so eagerly embraced and developed throughout that century, has resulted in the highest peaks of the modern city being declared off limits to the general public. These private spaces are the antithesis of civic-minded design, making the contemporary high rise a dramatic yet also sinister statement, the activities within its lofty peaks jealously shielded from view. The summits of some of the world's tallest and most spectacular buildings remain off limits to Everyman, and not just on account of security concerns. From the executive lounges at the peaks of Cesar Pelli's Petronas Towers in Kuala Lumpur to the glazed dome of Foster & Partners' 30 St Mary Axe, these are spaces which ordinary people can look at, but never touch.

Dystopias are far more dramatic and Hollywood's futurists continue to demonstrate seductive visions of nightmarish tomorrows. Just as the glamorous penthouse apartments of the 1920s and 1930s were recreated as gravity-defying sets for musicals and early talkies, so the futuristic roofscapes of tomorrow are the location for all manner of social commentary. Steven Spielberg's 2002 film *Minority Report*, based on Philip K Dick's short story, depicted apartment buildings with integrated vertical roads, and 'cars' (designed in conjunction with the Japanese manufacturer Lexus) that could dock with your sitting room, becoming an extension of your home.

In films, the penthouse is the peak of an architectural class system. The opening credits of Danny Cannon's 1995 film *Judge Dredd* (based on the comic strip in *2000AD* magazine) showed the lawless 'ground level' of Mega-City One, above which the lucky few take a dip in their rooftop pools. Luc Besson's *Fifth Element* went further, portraying a cliff-like Manhattan island raised high by plunging sea levels, adding another dimension to the famous street grid. Ordinary, everyday lives are lived in cramped, overlooked apartment buildings, while the heights are reserved for the city's more prosperous (and nefarious) characters. In a dystopic future of slowly accreted architectural and technological development, first demonstrated in Ridley Scott's iconic *Blade Runner* (1982), the penthouse – be it office or apartment – not only provided a haven from the mean, dark streets below but also allowed the cinematographer to showcase the roofscape, a device returned to again and again. In George Lucas's *Star Wars* prequel, *The Phantom Menace* (1999), the stately apartment of Queen Amidala is, effectively, a penthouse, all the better to showcase the surrounding city of Coruscant, created by the artist at Industrial Light and Magic. The cinema screen reduces the penthouse to little more than a view, a backdrop for the characters; the architecture itself is rarely a key generator for the plot.

The ultimate fictional exploration of the penthouse as the apotheosis of a new social order is the central conceit in JG Ballard's *High Rise*. Ballard was entranced by the new vertical estates so clearly visible from London's Westway and fused these with Le Corbusier's Unité d'Habitation, the vast apartment block in Marseilles that was intended to be a self-contained city block. As a result, he imagined a new vertical society, a middle-class paradise with a social structure carefully striated up and down its 40 floors. Atop all of this lived the high rise's architect, Anthony Royal, the building's first occupier, lording it over his domain from one of two penthouse apartments. Ballard's apartment dwellers were 'a new social type … a cool, unemotional personality impervious to the psychological needs of high-rise life, with minimal needs for privacy, who thrived like an advanced species of machine in the neutral atmosphere. This was the sort of resident who was content to do nothing but sit in his over-priced apartment, watch television with the sound turned down and wait for his neighbours to make a mistake …' The high rise was society in microcosm, social climbing played out for real, with class uprising taking a similarly literal path.

Klein Penthouse (unbuilt) LOT-EK

LOT-EK's best-known rooftop project is the Guzman Penthouse in midtown New York. Constructed partly from a reclaimed truck container, it is an iconic image of Modernism returned to its industrial roots mixed with the spirit of Post-Modern reappropriation and New York's famously bohemian loft culture. The project included extensive technological gadgets, most notably a vertically placed video monitor connected to a surveillance camera with a permanent view of the Empire State Building – a view of a view.

The firm's Klein Penthouse was an unbuilt concept for a photographer with a site in New York's Meat Packing District. Set atop the large flat expanse of a relatively low-rise building, the project again took the shipping container as the central architectural element. On this occasion, however, rather than inserting the container into an existing building, the rooftop was to be reconfigured to reflect the container's decidedly nonstatic origins.

The roofscape was to be laid out with six lanes, mimicking a parking lot. White kerbs separated each lane, and the roofing membrane was composed of black outdoor rubber granules. Three irregularly spaced zones – one each of grass, pebbles and water – formed the landscaping, while the accommodation took the shape of an 8 metre (26 foot) long truck container connected directly to the photographer's studio on the floor below.

Flower Tower Bill Dunster Architects Zedfactory Limited

It has been successfully demonstrated that the environmentally friendly skyscraper is no longer an oxymoron. Office towers by Ken Yeang and Norman Foster, among others, have shown that building tall can be energy efficient. However, there are currently few, if any, residential equivalents. Bill Dunster, architect of the low-energy BedZed development just outside London, has created the Flower Tower, a speculative, low cost, high-density block. Dunster's proposed innovations include a facade containing wind turbines and photovoltaic cells, a water-recycling system and communal sixth-floor gardens. The tower's floor plan is arranged as four petals radiating from a central spine, maximising light to the apartments, reducing wind-loading and improving heating and ventilation efficiency. The Flower Tower is an attempt to create mass-market high-rise housing, showing that perhaps, in the future, the penthouse won't be only the preserve of the super-rich.

Above [the middle section], on the top five floors of the high-rise, was its upper-class, the discreet oligarchy of minor tycoons and entrepreneurs, television actresses and careerist academics, with their high-speed elevators and superior services, their carpeted staircases. It was they who set the pace of the building. It was their complaints which were acted upon first, and it was they who subtly dominated life within the high-rise, deciding when the children could use the swimming-pools and roof garden, the menus in the restaurant and the high charges that kept out everyone but themselves. Above all, it was their subtle patronage that kept the middle ranks in line, this constant dangling carrot of friendship and approval.[2]

Although Ballard was clearly finding precedents in the work of Le Corbusier and Ernö Goldfinger (whose Trellick Tower in west London suffered high-profile crime problems in its early years), perhaps the closest match for

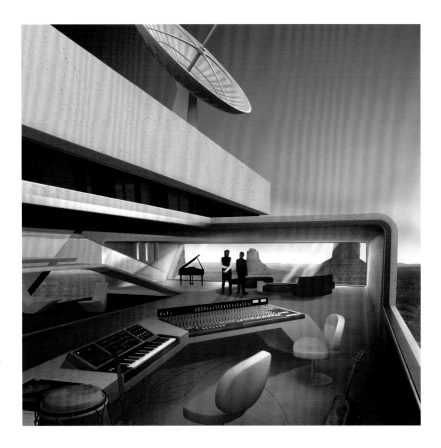

Opposite and right: **Mesa-Top Penthouse.**
Parisian designer Ora-Ito created this for the cover
art for Air's album *10,000Hz Legend*. It's a suitably
fanciful and futuristic space for the chic band,
furnished with vintage musical equipment,
communications equipment and the best views
imaginable

Ballard's vision is Johannesburg's Ponte City, designed by Rodney
Grosskopff in 1975. At 173 metres (575 feet) one of the tallest residential
buildings in the city, the Ponte's fortunes slid in the post-apartheid era. The
Brutalist structure – a giant cylinder of apartments overlooking a central light
well – apparently became a popular haunt of Nigerian crime lords and the
building swiftly descended into near anarchy; armed guards stood at the
entrance and rubbish piled up in the hollow core. At one point, local media
even suggested that the tower should become a high-rise prison. Atop it all
are six triple-height penthouses, truly fortresses in the sky, their faded
glamour unable to transcend their abject surroundings.

If dystopias lurk under the surface, and utopias struggle to get off the
ground, could not more pragmatic solutions prevail? The lure of living on high
invites the spectacular and, for the most part, excludes the utilitarian and
inclusive. Expensive technologies might show early promise but are inevitably
adopted for more exclusive ends. A good example of this is the role of the
helicopter in high-rise architecture. Initially seen as a saviour of urban
developers, a logical development of the tower crane, the helicopter (and, to
a certain extent, the airship) was envisioned as a tool for good by far-sighted
architects – reaching into the previously inaccessible nooks and crannies of
the city, dispensing a lightweight, super-practical and, above all, affordable
architecture. The new machine offered the promise of instant gratification,

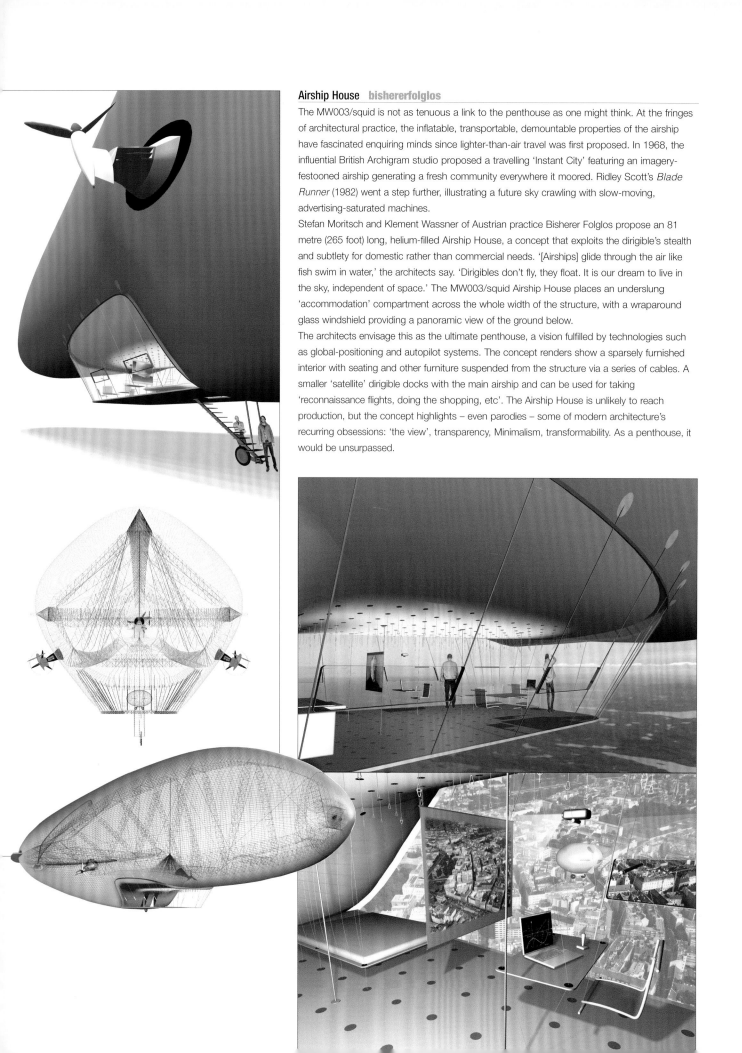

Airship House   bishererfolglos

The MW003/squid is not as tenuous a link to the penthouse as one might think. At the fringes of architectural practice, the inflatable, transportable, demountable properties of the airship have fascinated enquiring minds since lighter-than-air travel was first proposed. In 1968, the influential British Archigram studio proposed a travelling 'Instant City' featuring an imagery-festooned airship generating a fresh community everywhere it moored. Ridley Scott's *Blade Runner* (1982) went a step further, illustrating a future sky crawling with slow-moving, advertising-saturated machines.

Stefan Moritsch and Klement Wassner of Austrian practice Bisherer Folglos propose an 81 metre (265 foot) long, helium-filled Airship House, a concept that exploits the dirigible's stealth and subtlety for domestic rather than commercial needs. '[Airships] glide through the air like fish swim in water,' the architects say. 'Dirigibles don't fly, they float. It is our dream to live in the sky, independent of space.' The MW003/squid Airship House places an underslung 'accommodation' compartment across the whole width of the structure, with a wraparound glass windshield providing a panoramic view of the ground below.

The architects envisage this as the ultimate penthouse, a vision fulfilled by technologies such as global-positioning and autopilot systems. The concept renders show a sparsely furnished interior with seating and other furniture suspended from the structure via a series of cables. A smaller 'satellite' dirigible docks with the main airship and can be used for taking 'reconnaissance flights, doing the shopping, etc'. The Airship House is unlikely to reach production, but the concept highlights – even parodies – some of modern architecture's recurring obsessions: 'the view', transparency, Minimalism, transformability. As a penthouse, it would be unsurpassed.

elevating architecture to a new viewpoint. Buckminster Fuller's lightweight dome, Matti Suuronen's Futuro House, Richard Horden's Ski-haus, the work of Archigram, right through to Studio Aisslinger's LoftCube, all use the promise of instant delivery to site, regardless of location, the simplicity and practicality of prefabrication melded with the helicopter's lifting ability.

The helicopter didn't just play a supporting role during construction; it was the perfect mode of transport for tomorrow's world. Although various fictional futures developed this theme, envisaging means of transport that would use the new city's verticality as a way of saving time (Fritz Lang's *Metropolis* depicted huge aeroplanes making stately progress through the city's canyon-like streets), the helicopter promised to integrate transport into high-rise architecture, a potentially perfect combination that has remained elusive and impractical ever since. In February 1951, the American magazine *Popular Mechanics* conceived a suburb of tomorrow, complete with garages full of personal, commuter-helicopters. Similar futures were being planned for high rises. Indeed, concepts like Geoffrey Jellicoe's Motopia of 1961 showed housing located beneath a grid of roads, with helipads on key intersections for longer journeys.

But the apotheosis of that vision – the personal helipad fully integrated into the terraces of a penthouse home – remained a fantasy. Instead, it was the corporate world that embraced the romance and drama of the idea, while it was the emergency services who actually put it to practical good use. Ironically, the penthouse city, New York, presented such a complex and varying roofscape that the integration of helicopter transport never really took off, if the pun may be excused. Hybrid vehicles like the vast Fairey Rotodyne (1957) were designed specifically to operate short, commuter routes (the Airfix model of the Rotodyne showed it in front of London's Tower Bridge). Big corporate structures incorporated helipads, most notably Emery Roth & Sons' 1963 PanAm building in New York (now the Metlife), designed in conjunction with Walter Gropius and Pietro Belluschi. Two years after it opened, New York Airways started a helicopter shuttle service to JFK Airport, a jet-set offering with dramatic urban and rooftop views for the lucky passenger. It wasn't economic, however, and soon closed. The service started again in 1977, but was effectively ended by a catastrophic crash in May of that year which killed four passengers and an unfortunate passer-by, 246 metres (805 feet) below. As a result, few cities now embrace the helicopter's social potential, choosing instead to use it for emergency situations only. Californian building codes require structures over a certain height to incorporate a helipad at their summit, while air ambulances are a common sight in major cities.

Despite these futuristic dreams, the elevator is the only building technology the penthouse has ever needed. Penthouses still spearhead new developments, the word alone having the power to lift a whole development. 'Penthouse prices are set to go sky high!' read articles in the property press, as lofty apartments, costing many millions of pounds, become the focal point of new residential towers from Manchester to São Paulo, their interiors fitted out by big-name designers, their terraces landscaped by celebrity gardeners. Penthouses are the preserve of reality television shows, supplanting the lusted-after lofts of previous years as the most desired form of housing, or the apartment most befitting a pop star wannabe or aspiring model. A penthouse can top everything from a Nash terrace to a glass and steel tower, no longer referring to the very uppermost part of a building. Manhattan Loft's West India Quay, London's tallest residential building, designed by HOK, promises to provide the capital with its most spectacular penthouses, triplex glass structures on the 31st, 32nd and 33rd floors. A little further along the Thames, SOM's New Providence Wharf offers a cascade of penthouse apartments, some with their own pool, stepping down to the river.

The penthouse remains at the forefront of popular aspiration. London's building boom has given it what a city like New York had all along, a penthouse culture. New apartments and conversions of existing warehouses are suddenly everywhere, and none is complete without a penthouse, the key selling point in a ferocious market. Living in a penthouse implies a certain familiarity with a high, if not always flattering public profile. London taxi drivers point out Jeffrey Archer's penthouse in London's Vauxhall, a prominent, double-height space overlooking the Thames, which affords tantalising glimpses of large potted plants and walls dotted with artworks. Another famous peer's perch is Lord Foster's self-built space atop Riverside One, the speculative apartment building that houses the triple-height Foster & Partners studio on the ground floor. Foster's own apartment, complete with mature trees on the balcony, teeters on the edge of south London, looking north over the Thames. Next door, the firm has designed an altogether curvier contemporary apartment block, Albion Riverside, crowned, as usual, by double-height spaces.

The penthouse is simultaneously exhibitionist and isolated, hidden from prying eyes yet demanding attention. Perhaps more than any other form of modern architecture, the penthouse provides light, air, space and, critically, drama and glamour. Although roofs offer fresh real estate in cities that have run out of room, dreams of democratising this acreage in the air could be forever thwarted by the nature of the property market. Successful high-rise living has always been tantalisingly out of reach for the masses, presented only as the ultimate fantasy, the peak of architectural aspiration.

Notes
1   MVRDV, *FARMAX*, 010 Publishers (Netherlands), 1998.
2   JG Ballard, *High Rise*, Jonathan Cape (London), 1973, p 53.

Opposite and above: **New Providence Wharf.** A
new residential development in London's Docklands,
designed by the American super-practice of SOM.
The curving structures, which rise from 11 to 18
storeys, culminate in a series of spectacular
penthouses, totally integrated into the design

Residence Mumbai

SITE Environmental Architecture

Mumbai, India 2003

Traditionally, the penthouse represents an apex, drawing a considerable proportion of its prestige from the simple fact of its lofty supremacy over the other dwellings in the same building, a combination of proximity to the centre of a city, with all its connotations of power, glamour and practicality, and a commanding view over that same space, a view which implies ownership or mastery. A penthouse conveys more prestige than a similarly sized town house or detached private dwelling.

In this unbuilt residential scheme for Mumbai, India, SITE proposed a striking blend of the two, a single-family residential tower. Private high rises are extremely rare; there are only a few historical precedents, for example, the fortified towers of San Gimignano in Italy, where the brick structures, dating from the 13th century, were symbols of family prestige as well as protection from ongoing feuds, fights and kidnappings. Thankfully, domestic architecture rarely needs to demonstrate such agressive security. While many tycoons, speculators and captains of industry have lent their names to skyscrapers, and perhaps even live on the prestigious penthouse floors, residential occupancy of the entire structure is atypical.

Building high remains prestigious. Residence Mumbai is vast, nearly 27,870 square metres (300,000 square feet). Combining the principles of Vedic architecture – essentially the fusion of the disciplines of science, landscape and ecology – with allusions to the historical antecedent of the Hanging Gardens of Babylon, along with SITE's long history of environmentally friendly designs, the residence is a modern wonder. Recent projects by the New York-based studio, founded in 1970 by James Wines, build on the firm's reputation for visual eclecticism and wit (like the 'crumbling' stores designed for the BEST chain, or the 'ghost parking lot' of 1977), adding a rich layer of vegetation. SITE's current projects are characterised by a fascination with landscape, manmade and artificial, and the confluence of the two, as buildings emerge from naturally inspired landscaping and formal areas give way to carefully orchestrated chaos.

The upper living pavilion of Residence Mumbai is 150 metres (492 feet) above sea level, supported by a structural spine that also bears a cascading series of garden platforms in five symbolic floor stages, representing earth, water, fire, air and sound, with the upper three levels of the living space representing light and knowledge. Greenery is everywhere: in gardens, trellises and mazes; and in carefully devised settings for fountains, pools, sanctuaries, pavilions, outdoor dining spaces, sauna, Jacuzzi, sculpture, tearooms, dance

Above: Residence Mumbai. Design sketch of this ambitious scheme for a private skyscraper. Soaring more than 150 metres (490 feet) above downtown Mumbai, the residence is both structurally innovative and environmentally sound

Above: Residence Mumbai. A detail of one of the garden floors in this multilevel space. Arranged over five main levels symbolising earth, water, fire, air and sound, the project is characterised by the abundance of greenery

Right: **Residence Mumbai.** On different levels up the structure, pavilions are arranged to provide varying residential and entertainment functions, each set within a miniature landscape

Below: **Residence Mumbai.** The summit, and a view to end all views: Mumbai's skyline with the ocean beyond

floors and verandas, giving the building the appearance of a vertical forest.

At the summit is the main residence, a glass-walled pavilion that overlooks Mumbai's skyline and the ocean. A helipad provides easy access (an ironic counterpoint, perhaps, to the wealth of energy-saving features incorporated into the design).

The residence is a true vertical fantasy, albeit a technically possible one, the penthouse ideal cascading down to create a verdant tower, a symbol of extreme wealth and success that draws upon local tradition, science fiction visions and current environmental principles.

Above: Residence Mumbai. The entire project, illustrating how each different floor section is arranged around a central core and braced with structural rods on the perimeter of the floor plan. The upper floor, complete with cantilevered helipad, overhangs the rest of the residence

Above: Residence Mumbai. Each level is designed to feel wholly self-contained. The verdant surroundings are complemented by plenty of water features, illustrating the architect's embracing of a green architecture from both a technical and a spiritual standpoint

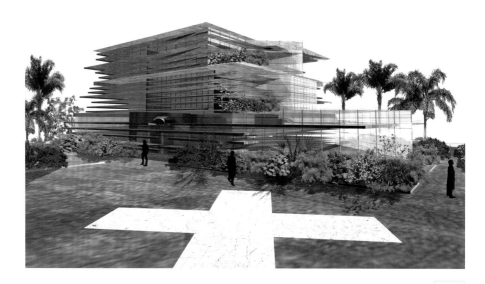

Right: Residence Mumbai. The topmost level is equipped with a helipad to provide easy access, somewhat at odds with the overt environmental approach

Bankside Paramorph

dECOi Digital Design Group

London 2004

The Bankside Paramorph is a penthouse oddity, a genuinely experimental project in method, material and construction. Mark Goulthorpe's dECOi Digital Design Group made its name with a series of highly speculative digital projects, virtual environments that subverted the traditional parameters of architectural space. Goulthorpe and his team have developed a series of computer-modelling processes, allowing conventional building techniques to be supplemented by computer-controlled modelling and cutting and using 'elastic' materials like fibreglass to physically manifest complex shapes.

Described as a complex, spiralling, tessellated enclosure, the Bankside Paramorph tops the round tower at Bankside Lofts, a prominent riverside apartment complex adjacent to Tate Modern, developed by the Manhattan Loft Corporation. The proposal wraps the existing structure with metal, glass and fabric, the structure held together by fibreglass trusses with inset glass panels and resin-filled aluminium honeycombs, a method that allows the structure also to provide weatherproofing and insulation.

dECOi's approach is twofold. Firstly, to continue the spiral form of the original curved tower, the Paramorph rests upon the existing stepped-ziggurat format of the tower's upper floors, currently arranged as a striking penthouse apartment. Viewed from the ground or the Millennium Bridge, the new structure appears simultaneously parasitic and integral to the existing building. The other intention is to maximise the thermal and structural efficiency, demonstrating that the myriad parameters offered by computer modelling and manufacturing can respond to literally any site, anywhere – the requirements of client, structure, planner, geography, location, climate, etc., generate the form.

Goulthorpe has a professorship at MIT where he leads the Design Group. The experimental nature of his work makes the penthouse a particularly pertinent building form, simultaneously prominent and concealed, a new layer of the city upon which to experiment.

Above: **Bankside Paramorph.** Viewed from the north bank of the Thames, this computer-generated image of the Bankside Paramorph shows the new structure emerging from the Bankside Lofts tower

Right: **Bankside Paramorph.** A closer view of the proposed Paramorph structure, which wraps itself around the existing stepped, circular tower

The Bankside scheme has two smaller-scale precursors in London. dECOi's Luschwitz/Bremner House was the proposed reconstruction of a Chelsea town house. Budget restraints ended the project, although permission was granted (despite a neighbour describing it as 'too contemporary'; the neighbour was Paloma Picasso). The engineers were Ove Arup (who also worked on the Bankside project). The Chelsea house was ostensibly about the creation of a new conservatory, albeit one which was designed to 'rumple' as it wrapped the corner of the building, the 'creases' making the glass structurally stable. Another penthouse, this in the shadow of St Paul's Cathedral, seems to grow organically from the roof, spilling out between the tall chimneys of the existing structure like a giant blob of mercury.

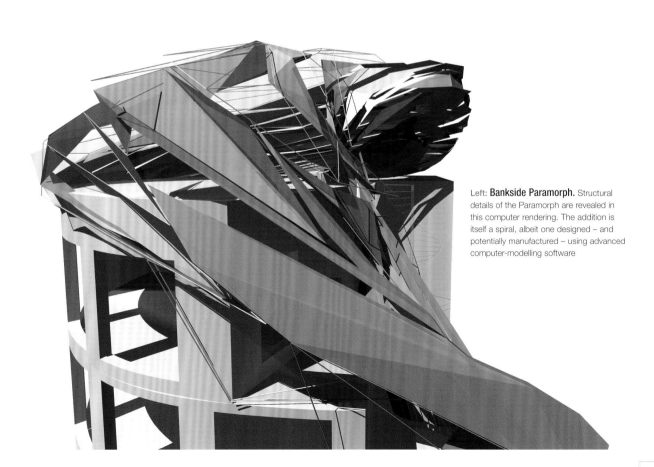

Left: **Bankside Paramorph.** Structural details of the Paramorph are revealed in this computer rendering. The addition is itself a spiral, albeit one designed – and potentially manufactured – using advanced computer-modelling software

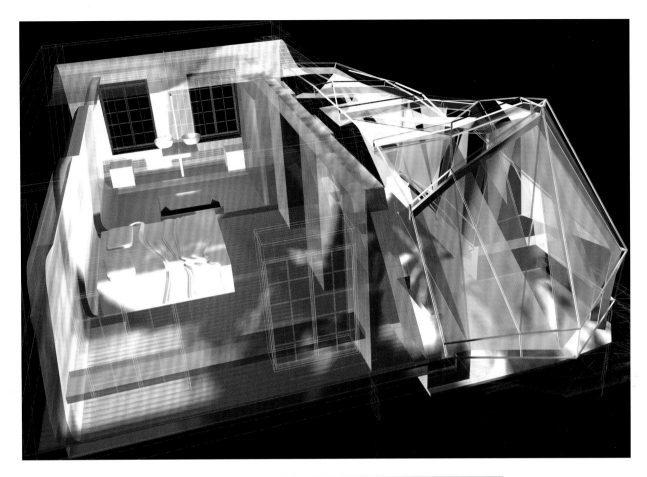

Above: The bedroom in the Luschwitz House, an earlier dECOI project that uses similar themes of parasitic, geometric enhancements to more conventional architectural space

Opposite and right: **Bankside Paramorph.** Three more views of the proposed structure

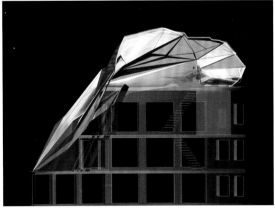

Docklands Penthouse

Richard Hywel Evans Architecture and Design Limited
London 2003

The Icon Building is a classic product of London's Docklands housing boom. The building was sold off-plan at the turn of the millennium but the developers' glossy pre-production images bore little resemblance to the draughty shells in which prospective owners eventually found themselves. In 2001, the hexagonal penthouse space was purchased by a bachelor businessman, a banker. The 10th-floor shell was in a parlous state, unfinished and uninhabitable. The roof was coated in AstroTurf to provide a makeshift putting green with a view, but this was probably the most dramatic touch in an otherwise pedestrian space. The banker employed the London-based firm of Richard Hywel Evans Architecture and Design, having been impressed by the practice's commitment to unusual, organic forms in its other works. His brief was simple – to 'make it like no other space I have ever walked into'.

Unsurprisingly, the finished result has an otherworldly quality. RHE's first task was to render the space mysterious, stripping out the existing partitions and imposing a series of curves and vistas. Key functions are divided up into pod-like sectors, an effect exploited by a series of blobby 'service rafts' which hang suspended from the existing ceiling. These rafts don't just define the flow of the space, they also act to diffuse light from the ceiling-mounted lighting system. Through the use of prominent curves in the flooring, ceiling, screens and custom-built furniture, RHE has delineated a series of zones for each of the key functions – living, sleeping, bathing, eating – without sacrificing the essentially open-plan nature of the apartment. Each zone also contains an item that defines its function, cunningly built into the space between the window openings. A plasma-screen television dominates the relaxation area, which also houses a concealed drinks cabinet, raised electronically at the push of a button.

This is a penthouse designed to dazzle and confuse, a true bachelor pad where the technological bounty of 21st-century living – the television, state-of-the-art fish tank and telescope for exploiting the lofty position – is prominently displayed. The wide range of materials used – leather, wood, aluminium stainless steel, silk, glass, walnut – coupled with the device of evenly spacing windows right around the apartment, sets up a series of evocative, almost confusing reflections, blending the bright lights of London's second financial district with the complex, multihued interior lighting system. Lighting is treated as another material, adding solidity or weightlessness to components at the twirl of a dial (like the underlit bedside tables, which appear to float). The bathroom is located behind a curving screen of translucent acrylic rods. Here

Above: Docklands Penthouse. A detail of the translucent screen concealing the bathroom area

Opposite: Docklands Penthouse. The main living space, with its futuristic, custom-made leather sofa, the 'service rafts' suspended from the ceiling and that classic bachelor pad accoutrement, the plasma-screen TV

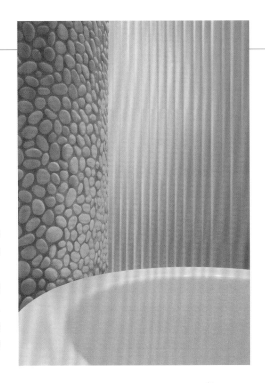

Right: **Docklands Penthouse.** The bathroom is a playful combination of artificial materials – translucent screens and pebble-effect cladding

the designers' imaginations have gone into overdrive, producing features like the pebble-effect-clad pillar, plastic floor and grey slates. Even the drab AstroTurf terrace has been enhanced with a barbecue and Jacuzzi.

It's not hard to source the inspirations behind this cinematically rich and glossy apartment. Penthouses and extravagance are frequently associated. Perhaps it's the height and the dizziness and playfulness created by gaining an unexpected perspective on one's surroundings, or maybe it's the sense that a penthouse is something to be lived up to, and not played down.

Left: **Docklands Penthouse.** The kitchen space, viewed from the counter, illustrating how the existing shell has been supplemented and enhanced by the addition of new, futuristic materials

Left: **Docklands Penthouse.** The main living space, clearly showing the blobby 'service pods' that hang above the main space and conceal the lighting systems

Above: **Docklands Penthouse.** Plan of the four distinct zones – living, sleeping, bathing and eating – that make up the apartment

Above: **Docklands Penthouse.** The dining area, with its single, streamlined support, reflects RHE's fascination with organic forms and the design of cars and boats

Below: **Docklands Penthouse.** Detail of the dining table and bench from the main living area, bespoke components designed specifically for this space

Below: **Docklands Penthouse.** Floor plan, showing how the organic spaces have been carved out of a conventional octagonal floor plan

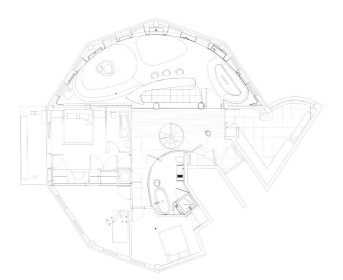

Haus Ray 1

Delugan Meissl Architects

Vienna, Austria 2003

The entirely individualistic contemporary penthouse is a rare beast. In a market saturated with pale imitators of the original classic apartments, where every second unit seems to have penthouse pretensions, finding a true original is unusual. Yet Haus Ray 1 is just that, an almost cinematically dramatic penthouse located atop a 1960s office building in Vienna. Viennese architects Delugan Meissl have created their own striking living space above a building close to the firm's own office. While it's also their home, Roman Delugan and Elke Delugan-Meissl created the penthouse apartment as a showcase fantasy, a three-dimensional brochure for the firm's spatial, structural and planning skills.

Haus Ray 1, named after the couple's young daughter Nora Ray, is a two-bedroom apartment with twin terraces and a pool. Nothing is conventional. The original office, with its blue facade, provides a formal base that is wholly transformed by its new addition. Access from the existing structure is through a new cantilevered stair that sticks out at right angles some 6 metres (20 feet) above the glass stair blocks of the existing circulation, providing views outwards across the city from a slot at floor level.

The architects have turned every possible view into a dramatic vista by a combination of unusually shaped window openings and careful framing. A giant structural steel framework was constructed atop the office's flat roof, 52 tons of angles, ramps and overhangs. The strength of the new structure allows the new penthouse space to be large, unsupported and open plan, a fact emphasised by the use of angled wall and floor planes, insertions that don't quite cross a span or fulfil the structural role that they initially appear to do.

The master bedroom, to the left of the entrance corridor, is perhaps the most dramatic internal space. The room is dominated by the cantilevered bed, which faces out of the sloping glass windows across the cityscape. The window 'sill' widens to encompass the sunken bath, another ostentatious gesture. The edges of the bathtub are picked up by the line of the walls and ceiling; every element is treated as if it is carved from a solid block – in this case Corian, a blend of acrylic and natural materials.

The main living space can be opened up to the terrace by means of sliding glass, frameless doors. A lap pool is sunk into the terrace, preserving the line of the floor level, with an 'infinity pool' effect at its edge, producing the effect of an apartment that merges into the city. The raised kitchen has units which rise from the floor, indistinguishable from the floor ramps and the external aluminium composite-clad frame, which becomes a ribbon winding around

Above: **Haus Ray 1.** The master bed is fused with the dramatic architecture of the penthouse, angled to look across the Viennese rooftops

Opposite: **Haus Ray 1.** Sliding glass doors open on to the terrace, which blends seamlessly into the pool, itself merging with the city skyline. The use of glass and steel is reminiscent of the Californian Case Study programme. The kitchen, with its wraparound counter, envelops the user and integrates all major functions in one long strip

the apartment's terraces and facades. The sloping roofscape created by the architects mimics, albeit the effect is achieved in a wholly different way, the mansard roofs and garrets of the slowly evolving European city.

Transformable elements, such as the desk which folds up into the angular run of cupboards, turn the entire wall into a series of sculptural – and bewildering – forms. The master bathroom is partitioned off by custom-designed glass screens and the shower is lit by a series of elongated portholes. Elsewhere, Expressionist bookshelves echo the angular lines of the outside roof, and the whole experience culminates in a leather-upholstered 'relaxation zone', with an uninterrupted view of the city, complete with that classic symbol of contemporary luxury, the overhead projector.

Above: **Haus Ray 1.** Viewed from a distance. The addition is dramatically different from the office building on which it sits

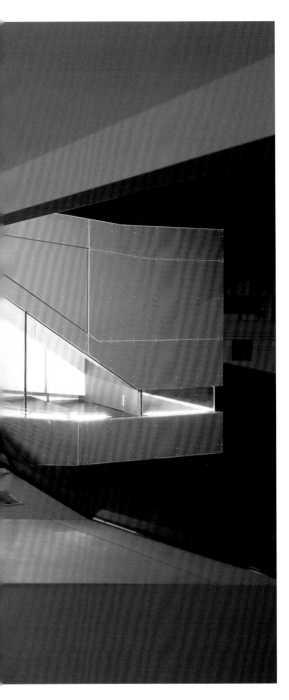

Below: **Haus Ray 1.** A general view of the terrace and dining area, showing the combination of right angles and large planes of glass

Above: **Haus Ray 1.** The master bed at night, showing its cantilevered structure

Above: **Haus Ray 1.** Looking back in on the apartment, showing the terrace beside the pool and the dining area

Opposite: **Haus Ray 1.** The external terrace, showing the balustrade that snakes around the entire apartment

TO's Place

pool Architektur

Vienna, Austria 1999

A tiny shelter on the roof of an existing building, TO's Place is the antithesis of the grand interwar penthouse and an exemplary model of the contemporary desire to explore the unknown roofscape. The owner, Johannes Rudnicki bought a site that previously comprised just a water tank, an 18 square metre (194 square feet) space with very little obvious potential.

Florian Wallnöfer of Vienna-based firm pool Architektur carved up the existing area and exploited the awkward dynamics of the rising staircase and the limitations of the one-room space. Essentially, all the key functions are designed to fold or slide away or to be so minimally detailed as to fade away in everyday use. There is just a single main living space which is opened up to the elements by a pair of vast folding glass doors. It is served by a small toilet, complete with swivelling television set (so it can serve both spaces) built into the wall.

The kitchen unit cantilevers off the slope created by the roof of the staircase. The angular black steel slab points to a high slot window, reminiscent of medieval castle design, that brings in a shaft of light, the only other available aspect. With a welcome touch of Surrealism, the fridge is suspended from the ceiling, a white cube that takes on a sculptural, uncanny quality. The master bed is cleverly recessed into the wall, sliding away flush to the wall surface when not in use. A writing desk also shares this alcove, effectively switching the space from bedroom to sitting room. Likewise, storage is contained within a large sliding storage cabinet, similarly recessed and designed to provide a privacy wall when extended out into the main space.

Bathing facilities are served by a simple shower tucked almost unnoticed into the corner of the room. The shower tray is recessed just beneath the level of the finished floor and the white basin sits unobtrusively against the white rendered, rough brick walls. The glass doors provide uninterrupted views on to the terrace, which is delineated by humble fencing ranging around its perimeter. A concrete slab runs from inside to out, unadorned and simple.

Fittings and finishes are simple and industrial, from the wall-mounted uplighters to the polished concrete floors. The project was built in just two months, at a remarkably low cost of €12,000. This is the penthouse as urban subversion – the best views snatched, guerrilla-style, by bold architectural experiments and the willingness to push the boundaries to the edge.

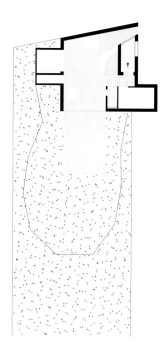

Above: **TO's Place.** The floor plan of this rooftop eyrie that perches precariously atop an existing building

Right: **TO's Place.** The internal fittings and fixtures are all built-in to maximise the tight floor plan. The kitchen unit cantilevers out from the sloping wall, its shape dictated by the stairwell below

Below: **TO's Place.** View from the terrace looking in. The white slab of concrete is the owner's minimal patio, a solid structure adrift in a sea of pea-shingle-strewn rooftop

Above: **TO's Place.** Transformability is the way to make such a small space work. The bed slides out of the way into the wall when not in use

Below: **TO's Place.** The wardrobe is a sliding element, and acts as a screen for the bed. When not in use, each item leaves behind its silhouette, flush with the plane of the wall

Above: **TO's Place.** Another view of the kitchen and
bathroom area. The shower is Minimalism incarnate
– a sloped floor to drain the water away and a
single head protruding from the wall

Right: **TO's Place.** Neat flexible touches
are everywhere; this shows the reversible
wall-mounted television – allowing for TV
in the WC as well as the main space

LoftCube

Studio Aisslinger

Berlin 2004

Studio Aisslinger's LoftCube combines the appeal of rooftop living with three other emerging trends: smaller living spaces, portable architecture and prefabrication. Essentially a square, caravan-like structure, the lightweight LoftCube is described as a 'mobile home for urban nomads'. First exhibited at Berlin's inaugural DesignMai festival in May 2003, LoftCube was based on architect Werner Aisslinger's desire to create a Minimalist, temporary retreat that was still a practical proposition for a dense inner-city location.

The spot chosen for the prototype, a former cold-storage depot overlooking the Spree River and now used as record company offices, is typical of many industrial sites – large expanses of flat roof going to waste. Aisslinger envisions the concept as functioning like an upscale hotel, a temporary home from home where like-minded people can spend short periods of time 'congregating in rooftop communities – floating on top of the city, yet being where the action is'. A LoftCube would cost around €55,000, but the price of a suitable site could be far higher.

Drawing on earlier housing concepts such as Pierre Botschi's 1973 moulded GRP 'mobile house', the LoftCube has a lightweight construction to maximise the number of sites for which it is suited. A structure of Bankirai wood is infilled with honeycomb panels, coated with a white laminate and specially developed plastic sheets; inside extensive use has been made of Corian to create a series of movable, transformable function panels. This means that the bath and kitchen share a tap, which can be swung between the two zones. The same goes for the shower and plant basin that separate the bathing and living areas. In this way, Aisslinger ensures that the LoftCube's living spaces appear much larger than they are, in keeping with the penthouse's traditional emphasis on space. Wall panels are constructed from translucent acrylic glass.

The association of the high life with high achievement is clear, if slightly tongue in cheek, yet the concept makes a more serious point about 'flying buildings', temporary architecture and transportability. The LoftCube, it is mooted, could be transported to its perch by freight helicopter (bringing to mind the iconic image of Buckminster Fuller's geodesic dome suspended beneath a Sikorsky S-55) or via a crane. The idea of a private rooftop society is also paradoxical, suggesting people who seek to remove themselves from the real world at street level, a development of the science fiction device of the socially layered city where height and security are inextricably linked.

Above: **LoftCube.** The internal fit-out makes extensive use of Corian, a hard-wearing combination of natural materials and acrylic polymer

Below: **LoftCube.** Interior view of the kitchen and
bathroom showing the transformable function
panels that divide the living spaces

Above: LoftCube. The flip side of this panel functions as the shower, with the shower head flipping through the panel to double up as a watering device for the plant

Above: LoftCube. Elements are as integrated as possible – right down to plant pots

Left: **LoftCube.** Wherever possible, panels have a dual function; this module holds the kitchen and bathroom sinks. The design updates the Japanese wood and paper house with modern materials

Below: **LoftCube.** The master bedroom, with its combination of transparent and translucent wall panels

Above left and right: **LoftCube.** LoftCube can be placed atop any structure, legal requirements permitting. It is the ultimate incarnation of the Modernist 'pavilion in the sky'

m-house

Tim Pyne
London 2002

Described as a 'meticulously designed, engineered and constructed contemporary building on wheels', the m-house is just one of several prefabricated building solutions aimed at both the urban and rural homeowner. Developed by the architect Tim Pyne, m-house is a classic pavilion, a refined version of the ubiquitous Portakabin or trailer. Designed to fall within the legal definition of a caravan, making siting far easier and less prone to the whims of Britain's notoriously unpredictable planning laws, it has the added advantage of a swift six-week delivery time.

The m-house makes a great virtue of its flexibility. Equally suited to a seaside caravan park, floating on a pontoon or, most importantly, a site on top of an existing building, the house is composed of a single 3 metre x 17 metre (10 x 56 feet) unit, which can be doubled up to create a far wider, more spacious structure. The specification, materials, fixtures and fittings are all equivalent – or superior – to those found in a high quality caravan or motor home and the emphasis has been placed on customising each individual unit to the client's own specification. Protective blinds double as awnings, folding down over the large, floor to ceiling windows to act as security.

The m-house attracted an enormous amount of interest – from second-homers, wannabe expatriates, families anxious to find space for ageing relatives, and caravan park owners looking to update their image. The dream of a semiportable, relatively affordable and well-finished prefabricated building has haunted architects for the best part of a century. Numerous solutions have been proposed, from the space-age Futuro House of the 1960s to contemporary work by American firms like Resolution: 4 Architecture. The idea of an instant rooftop pavilion overcomes the traditional barrier to penthouse living – the cost. Production of a lightweight structure that can be transported by crane or helicopter on to an existing flat roof is, perhaps, viewed as a democratic, almost subversive, act – a means of gaining wider access to previously hidden spaces.

Below: **m-house.** Internal fit-outs take their cue from upmarket caravan and yacht designs

Above: **m-house.** The main living/dining area is light and spacious, with 2.4 metre (eight foot) high ceilings throughout

Left above and below: **m-house.** The main space can be fitted out without internal walls, for use as an office or showroom

Opposite: **m-house.** The external metal skin

Superquadras Penthouses

Deckker Architects

Brasília 2004

Arguably the most famous Modernist roofscape is Le Corbusier's Unité d'Habitation in Marseilles. The 337 apartments, with space for up to 1,700 people, were served by an internal shopping street and a roof garden. Here one could find a children's playground and pool, a 300 metre (985 foot) long running track and a snack bar with a fashionable 'solarium'. Sculptural, rock-like shapes mirrored the distant mountains and the whole roof encapsulated Corbusier's early obsession with the ocean liner and how the summit of a vast superstructure could be utilised as a recreational area, with far-reaching views and maximum sunlight and air. Contemporary drawings compare the Unité skyline of chimneys, lift shafts, stairs and platforms with the liner's decks and funnels.

On the other side of the Atlantic, Corbusier's ideals were being realised on a much larger scale. Brasília, planned by Oscar Niemeyer and Lucia Costa, contained dedicated residential districts in the 'wings' that sprouted from the central axis of the city plan. These districts were known as Superquadras, integrating schools, shops and recreation areas along with a group of high-density housing units. The idea was to mix social classes and avoid the creation of slum housing. Some 92 Superquadras were planned and just 10 were completed by 1964, when the majority of the new city was deemed complete. Only six of these had the original landscaping and social facilities planned by Niemeyer and the landscape architect Roberto Burle Marx.

Brasília's housing needs were demanding and went largely unmet. The architectural emphasis on social engineering pointedly omitted working-class areas and makeshift housing created for the thousands of construction workers evolved into slums. Uncompleted areas of the city plan still lie empty. The architect Thomas Deckker attempted to address some of this 'leftover' space in his Superquadras penthouse project. Noting that these vast blocks, their facades lacking the modulation and variation that characterised Corbusier's Unité, had underutilised, 'architecturally incomplete' roof areas, Deckker set out to make the rooftops habitable.

Deckker draws an unexpected comparison between the Brazilian roofscapes and the shifting sand dunes of Blakeney Point on the Norfolk coast and the way the natural erosion of the sand is artificially stabilised by a series of wooden windbreaks. The haphazard arrangement of these stakes subdivides the barren landscape into a series of architecturally distinct elements. The Superquadras presented a similarly expansive landscape, one which could also be subdivided by architectural means.

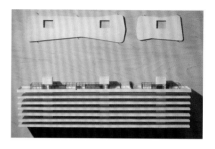

Above: **Superquadras Penthouses.** Elevational view of the Superquadras model

Below: **Superquadras Penthouses.** View of the top floor of the Superquadras, with the new spatial arrangement marked by the new cordons

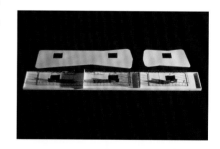

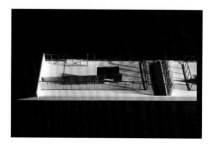

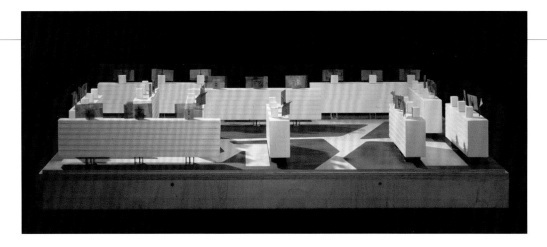

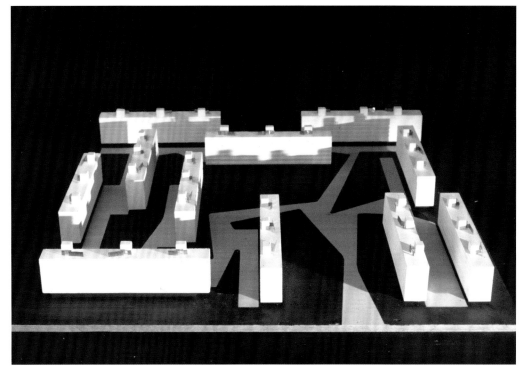

Above: **Superquadras Penthouses.** The vast scale of the Superquadras housing projects creates an enormous amount of unused space at roof level. Deckker's proposals aim to change the perception of these 'penthouse' spaces

Deckker's proposal is for a series of cordons to be built on the roofs of the Superquadras, 'a wall placed against each lift tower to define "front" and "back", or "social" and "service" sides'.

Deckker is explicit about the political dimension of the unbuilt project. By creating a varied and hierarchical social mix – the new upper layer would be 'necessarily for the more sophisticated' – the Superquadras project positions the penthouse firmly as an aspirational, exclusive dwelling, almost in diametrical opposition to the ideals of the building's original architects.

Web House

m³ Architects

London 2004

m³ architects Nadi Jahangiri, Ken Hutt and Ivy Chan believe in devising and prototyping avant-garde architectural schemes as a means of generating debate about the social changes architecture needs to address. Their scheme for a new eco-friendly hotel demonstrates that high-tech building can have an ultra-light touch on the environment, while their Spitalfields Tritower illustrated that large amounts of new office space were compatible with the retention of Spitalfields Market, subsequently half-demolished for a commercial scheme.

This architectural lateral thinking has led to the Web House, a conceptual dwelling that tackles the distinct lack of sites in central London. Challenging the orthodox wisdom – that a site should be 'a flat piece of unencumbered land' – the architects sought a new approach, democratising the search for affordable, centrally located space. Why not use existing structures? While the traditional penthouse is built on an empty roof, the Web House claims squatter's rights, clinging to the side of existing commercial and residential structures.

The Web House is true to its name, a construction that can be 'hung' anywhere, draped off the side of an existing building, slung in the gaps in the streetscape, across roads or over railway lines. Formed from an inflatable external skin, which is delivered to site in a package measuring just 3 cubic metres (106 cubic feet), the Web is mounted, inflated and then braced by a structural core, which also contains all the necessary service points and utilities plus a kitchen module. Services are drawn, parasite-like, from the existing building and access is provided by a wall-climbing external lift.

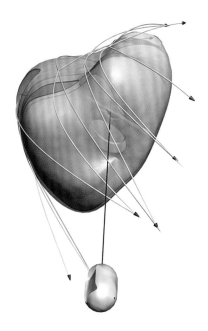

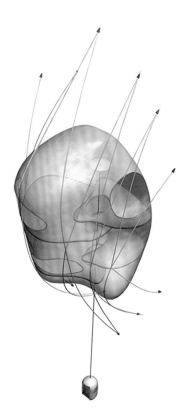

Above: **Web House**. The inflatable external 'skin' is attached to the host by means of a series of harness points, allowing it to be easily demounted

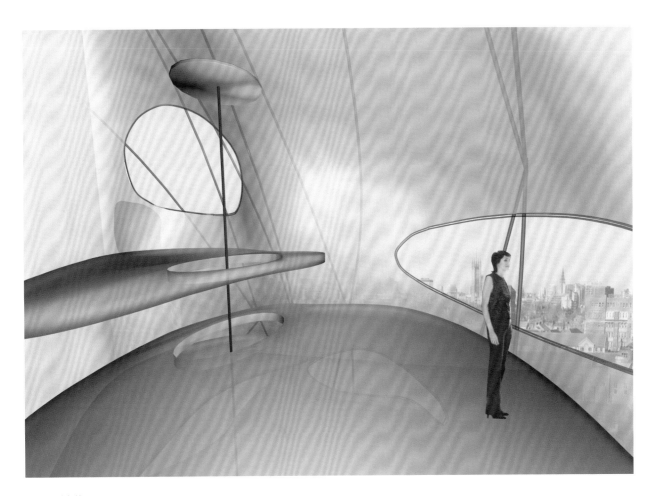

Above: **Web House.** From within, the 'host'
building is invisible, while organic forms and
openings reveal wide-ranging views

Right: **Web House.** It is designed to cling, parasite-
like, to the side of an existing building

Listings

London SW4 0BG, UK
Tel: 44.20 7501 0180
Fax: 44.20 7798 7103
www.skyhouse.co.uk
info@marksbarfield.com

Tim Pyne, m-house
31 Charlotte Road
London EC2A 3PB, UK
Tel: 44.20 7739 4553
Fax: 44.20 7739 4854
www.m-house.org
tim@m-house.org

m³ architects
74 Great Eastern Street
London EC2A 3JG, UK
Tel: 44.20 7729 4222
Fax: 44.20 7729 4333
www.m3architects.com
post@m3architects.com

Munkenbeck + Marshall Architects
135 Curtain Road
London EC2A 3BX, UK
Tel: 44.20 7739 3300
Fax: 44.20 7739 3390
www.mandm.uk.com

MVRDV
Schiehaven 15
3024 EC Rotterdam, The Netherlands
Tel: 31.10 477 2860
Fax: 31.10 477 3627
www.mvdrv.nl
mvrdv@archinet.com

OBR Architetti Associati
Piazza San Matteo 15
16123 – Genoa, Italy
Tel: 39.010 2518456
Fax: 39.010 2479469
www.openbuildingresearch.com

Ora-Ito
100 rue Folie Méricourt
75011 Paris, France
Tel: 33.1 42 46 00 09
Fax: 33.1 42 46 03 09
www.ora-ito.com

pool Architektur ZT GmbH
A-1040 Vienna, Austria
Weyringergasse 36/1
Tel: 43.1 503 82 31 -0
Fax: 43.1 503 82 31 33
http://pool.helma.at
fw@pool.helma.at

**Richard Hywel Evans Architecture and
Design Limited**
Great Titchfield House
14–18 Great Titchfield Street
London W1P 7AP, UK

Tel: 44.20 7436 3400
www.rhe.uk.com

Johannes Saurer Architekt
Freienhofgasse 11
3600 Thun, Switzerland
Tel: 41.33 221 08 48
Fax: 41.33 221 08 46
johannessaurer@datacomm.ch

Harry Seidler and Associates
Level 5, 2 Glen Street
Milsons Point
Sydney
New South Wales 2061, Australia
Tel: 61.2 9922 1388
Fax: 61.2 9957 2947
www.seidler.net.au
hsa@seidler.net.au

Siris/Coombs Architects
2112 Broadway, Suite 405
New York, NY 10023, USA
Tel: 1.212 580 2220
www.siriscoombs.com

SITE-Environmental Architecture
25 Maiden Lane, 2nd Floor
New York, NY 10038, USA
Tel: 1.212 285 0120
Fax: 1.212.285 0125
www.sitenvirondesign.com
sitejw@interport.net

SOM
1 Oliver's Yard
London EC1Y 1HH, UK
Tel: 44.20 7798 1000
Fax: 44.20 7798 1100
www.som.com

Stanton Williams Architects
Diespeker Wharf
38 Graham Street
London N1 8JX, UK
Tel: 44.20 7880 6400
Fax: 44.20 7880 6401
www.stantonwilliams.com

Studio Aisslinger
Werner Aisslinger
Oranienplatz 4
10999 Berlin, Germany
Tel: 49.30 3150 5400
www.aisslinger.de
werner@aisslinger.de

Tangram Architekten
Olympisch Stadion 8
1076 DE Amsterdam, The Netherlands
Tel: 31.20 676 1755
Fax: 31.20 676 8737
www.tangramarchitekten.nl

James Wagman Architect LLC
435 Hudson Street, 4th Floor
New York, NY 10014, USA
Tel: 1.212 337 9649
Fax: 1.212 337 9641
www.jameswagman.com
wagdg@aol.com

John Young/Richard Rogers Partnership
Thames Wharf
Rainville Road
London W6 9HA, UK
Tel: 44.20 7385 1235
Fax: 44.20 7385 8409
www.richardrogers.co.uk
enquiries@rrp.co.uk

ZEDfactory/Bill Dunster Architects
24 Helios Road
Wallington
Surrey SM6 7BZ, UK
Tel: 44.20 8404 1380
Fax: 44.20 8404 2255
www.zedfactory.com

COMMERCIAL VENUES

Claridge's
Brook Street
London W1A 2JQ, UK
Tel: 44.20 7629 8860
Fax: 44.20 7499 2110
www.claridges.co.uk
info@claridges.co.uk

The Dorchester Hotel
Park Lane
London W1A 2JH, UK
Tel: 44.20 7629 8888
Fax: 44.20 7409 0114
www.dorchesterhotel.com
info@dorchesterhotel.com

Kensington Roof Gardens
99 Kensington High Street
London W8 5ED, UK
Tel: 44.20 7937 7994
www.roofgardens.com

Bibliography

Abramson, Daniel M, *Skyscraper Rivals: The AIG Building and the Architecture of Wall Street*, Princeton Architectural Press (New York), 2001

Allan, John, *Berthold Lubetkin: Architecture and the Tradition of Progress*, RIBA Publications (London),1992

Alpern, Andrew, *New York's Fabulous Luxury Apartments with Original Floor Plans from the Dakota, River House, Olympic Tower and Other Great Buildings*, Dover Publications (New York), 1987

Ballard, JG, *High Rise*, Jonathan Cape (London), 1973

Fraser, Valerie, *Building the New World: Studies in the Modern Architecture of Latin America 1930–1960*, Verso (London), 2000

Louis Sullivan: The Function of Ornament, exhibition catalogue, Saint Louis Art Museum, 1986

Giedion, Siegfried, *Space, Time and Architecture*, Harvard University Press (Cambridge, Mass), third edition, 1956

Höweler, Eric, *Skyscraper: Designs of the recent past and for the near future*, Thames and Hudson (London), 2003

Ireson, Ally and Nick Barley (eds), *City Levels*, August/Birkhäuser (London), 2000

MVDRV, *FARMAX*, 010 Publishers (The Netherlands), 1998

Sanders, James, *Celluloid City*, Knopf (New York), 2001

Trager, James, *Park Avenue, Street of Dreams*, Atheneum (New York), 1990

Tzonis, Alexander, *Le Corbusier: The Poetics of Machine and Metaphor*, Thames and Hudson (London), 2001

Zukin, Sharon, *Loft Living: Culture and Capital in Urban Change*, Radius (London) 1998